Copyright © 1996 by Mary H. Ross and Jennette Guymon
All Rights Reserved

Covenant Communications, Inc.
American Fork, Utah

Printed in the United States of America
First Printing: January 1996

96 97 98 99 00 01   10 9 8 7 6 5 4 3 2

Primary Partners: Book of Mormon - Ages 8-11
ISBN 1-55503-906-5

PRIMARY PARTNERS

A- Z Activities
to Make Learning Fun

for Ages 8-11
Book of Mormon

46 Lesson Match Learning Activities ◪ Book of Mormon Activity Notebook Pages

Simple Supplies Needed ◪ Matching Thought Treats

46 Scripture Challenge Cards with Reward Glue-on Stickers

Use for Primary Lessons, Family Home Evening,

and Daily Devotionals to Reinforce Gospel Topics

You'll Find: A-Z Topics to Match Primary Lessons

Adversity   Armor of God   Baptism   Beatitudes   Book of Mormon
Charity   Choices   Choose the Right   Christmas   Commandments
Covenants   Easter   Eternal Life   Example   Faith   Forgiveness
Freedom   Happiness   Holy Ghost   Honor   Love   Missionary
Obedience   Prayer   Priesthood   Prophets   Repentance   Righteousness
Sacrament   Scriptures   Signs   Testimony   Truth   Trust   Worship

INTRODUCTION
PRIMARY PARTNERS:
Fun Learning Activities for Primary 4 Lessons
Book of Mormon Ages 8-11

Primary teachers and parents, you'll enjoy using the PRIMARY PARTNERS activities to supplement your Primary lessons, enhance your family home evenings, and help children learn gospel principles in fun, challenging ways. Children love these easy, fun-to-create visuals. Patterns for each project are actual size, ready to Copy-n-Create in minutes to make learning fun.

How to Use This Book

1. **Use the Lesson #1-46 Table of Contents** to match your lessons found in the Primary 4* manual.

2. **Preview A-Z Table of Contents** to find activities that match gospel subjects.

3. **Lesson Activities** coordinate with specific parts of the lesson. For example, Lesson #3 Commandments Concentration activity (pages 4-5) complements page 9 (Enrichment Activity #5) in the Primary 4 manual* (look for the box in each lesson, e.g., shown right).

> *Review Enrichment Activity #5 (page 9) in the Primary 4 manual*.*

4. **Copy Patterns Ahead.** You'll save time and avoid last minute preparation.

5. **Shop Ahead For Simple Supplies.** Each activity requires a few basic items: Copies of patterns, scissors, crayons, tape, glue, zip-close plastic bags, paper punch, yarn/ribbon, metal brads, pencils, and wooden craft sticks.

6. **Copy Patterns Ahead.** You'll save time and avoid last minute preparation.

7. **Organize Activities** A-Z for family home evening, or #1-46 for Primary lessons. Copy instructions to include with the pattern copies and supplies.

8. **Activity Journal:** Provide each child with a 3-ring binder or folder to store classroom creations. Encourage children to display activities in their room for a few weeks before placing them in their notebook. Include in all notebooks the "I'm Trying to Be Like Jesus" cover page (in the back of this book) with the child's picture next to Jesus. Children can fill in their personal goals and information.

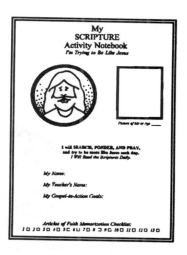

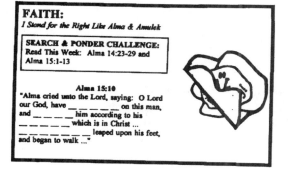

9. **Scripture Challenge Cards:** You'll find Scripture Challenge Cards to match lessons #1-46*.

♥ **Challenge Scripture Reading.** Assign a SCRIPTURE CHALLENGE CARD each week (see patterns on pages 91-114). Children can read the scriptures assigned and fill in the blanks on the featured scripture. ♥ **Reward for Scripture Reading.** As children bring the completed card the next week, reward them with a large glue-on sticker to match the image on the card. This larger sticker shows the children that their testimony grows as they read the scriptures. ♥ **Help Children Organize Cards.** Option #1: Create a book by punching holes in card tabs and lace or ring them together. See book cover label on page 91.

Option #2: Store cards in a zip-close plastic bag (cutting left tab off). Place the label in front of cards.

*Primary 4 manual is published by The Church of Jesus Christ of Latter-day Saints, Salt Lake City, Utah.

Primary Lessons #1-46 Table of Contents

*Primary 4 manual is published by The Church of Jesus Christ of Latter-day Saints, Salt Lake City, Utah.

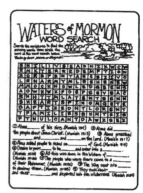

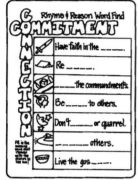

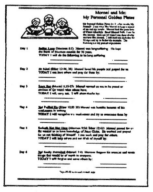

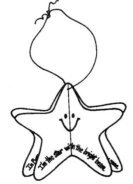

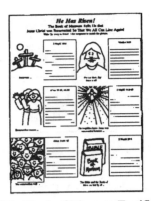

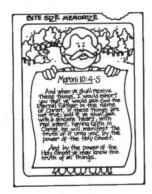

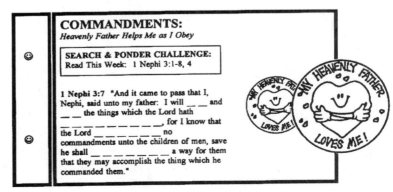

Lesson #1*	**BOOK OF MORMON:** Another Testament of Jesus *(reading challenge chart)*

YOU'LL NEED: Copy of Scripture Challenge card (page 92) and Book of Mormon Challenge reading chart (page 2) on cardstock paper for each child, glue, and crayons.

ACTIVITY: Help children learn the Book of Mormon Promise in Moroni 10:4-5 and challenge them to read the entire Book of Mormon.

Review Suggested Home Reading (page 3) in the Primary 4 manual*.

1. Children and teacher or parent can color in each chapter square after they have read that chapter.
2. Teacher or parent can check with children week after week, showing their own personal reading chart as an example.

SCRIPTURE CHALLENGE: Do activity in class or at home.

THOUGHT TREAT: Hill Cumorah Trees. Remind children of the hill where the Book of Mormon plates were buried and found hundreds of years later. Serve celery or broccoli trees.

Lesson #2*	**PROPHET:** I Will Follow the Living Prophet *(Wilderness Journey object find)*

YOU'LL NEED: Copy of Scripture Challenge card (page 92) and Wilderness Journey scene (page 3) on colored cardstock paper for each child, pencil, and crayons.

ACTIVITY: Strengthen each child's desire to follow the living prophet. Tell children to imagine

Review Discussion and Application Questions (page 6) in Primary 4 manual*.

going with Lehi and his family into the wilderness. Wilderness Journey Object Find. Help Lehi pack for his trip into the wilderness with his family. Find for him the following: bow, arrow, tent, sword, plate, spoon, fruit, water jug, meat, and a sack of grain.

SCRIPTURE CHALLENGE: Do activity in class or at home.

THOUGHT TREAT: Follow-the-Leader Lemonade. Make some fresh lemonade. Tell children, "When life gives you lemons, make lemonade." Write this saying on a lemon shaped straw decoration. Tell children that by following the prophet we can make sour lemon days sweet days. Listen to what the prophet and other church leaders say in general conference. Read their messages in the church magazines. Listen carefully to your Primary and family home evening lessons to make each day just that much sweeter.

| Lesson #3* | **COMMANDMENTS: Heavenly Father Helps Me as I Obey**
(Commandment Concentration) |

YOU'LL NEED: Copy Scripture Challenge card (page 93) and two sets of commandment match cards (page 5) on colored cardstock paper and a zip-close plastic bag for each guest, scissors, glue, and crayons.

ACTIVITY: Assemble a Commandment Concentration game for each child and place in an envelope or zip-close plastic bag to remind them of how they can obey the commandments to receive blessings from Heavenly Father.

Review Enrichment Activity #5 (page 9) in Primary 4 manual*.

TO MAKE AND PLAY GAME: Color and cut out card sets. Place cards face down. Each player turns two cards over to try to make a match. If cards match, keep matching cards. If cards don't match, turn cards back over and next player tries to make a match. Continue until last match is made.

SCRIPTURE CHALLENGE: Do activity in class or at home.

THOUGHT TREAT: <u>Commandment Chips</u>. Let children munch on potato chips as they play Commandment Concentration. Tell them that if we "chip" in and help ourselves and others obey the commandments, we will find true happiness.

| Lesson #4* | **ETERNAL LIFE: I Will Follow the Path to Heaven**
(3-D box with Tree of Life vision) |

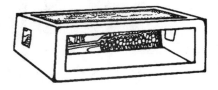

YOU'LL NEED: Copy Scripture Challenge card (page 93) and 3-D box (pages 6-7) on cardstock paper for each child, scissors, glue, and crayons.

Review Discussion and Application Questions (pages 13-14) in the Primary 4 manual*.

ACTIVITY: Create a three-dimensional box with the Tree of Life vision figures inside. Then look through the window to see the vision father Lehi had. As you view the contents, discuss how obeying the word of God will help us to be worthy of eternal life, so we can live with Heavenly Father and Jesus again (1 Nephi 8, 11, and 15:21-36). (1) Color and cut out box and scene pieces. (2) Fold box and pieces where indicated. (3) Glue pieces in place and then glue tabs to enclose box. (4) Glue label on top of box.

SCRIPTURE CHALLENGE: Do activity in class or at home.

THOUGHT TREAT: <u>Tree of Life Apple Slices</u>. Prepare apple slices before class. Remind children that the fruit of the tree of life is Eternal Life, which comes from living the gospel of Jesus Christ. Read: 1 Nephi 8:11.

Pray Daily

Partake of the Sacrament

Serve a Mission

Pay Tithing

Love Others

Read Scriptures

Attend the Temple

Obey the Word of Wisdom

PATTERN: *ETERNAL LIFE (3-D box to view Tree of Life vision)*

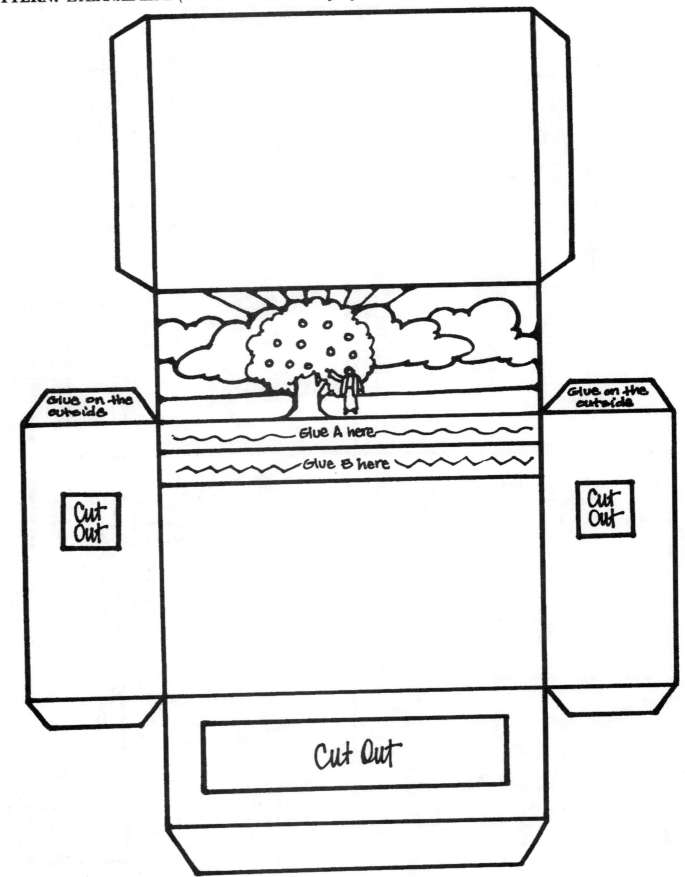

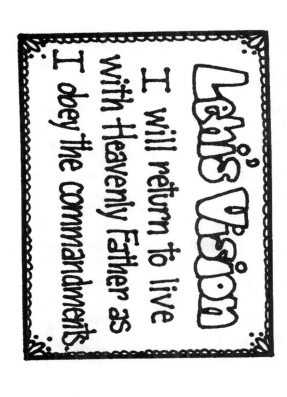

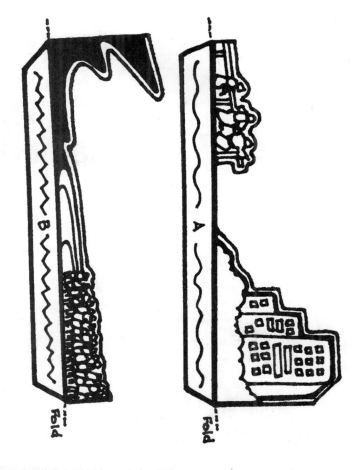

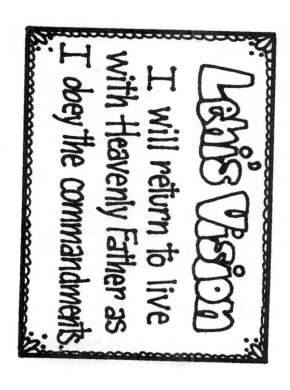

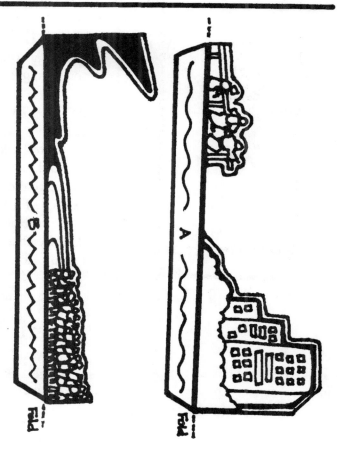

Lesson #5*	**TRUST: Heavenly Father Will Guide Me** *(Poster message 2 Nephi 4:15-24)*

YOU'LL NEED: Copy Scripture Challenge card (page 94) and poster message (page 9) on colored cardstock paper for each child, scissors, glue, and crayons.

ACTIVITY: Help children understand that they can trust in Heavenly Father and that he will guide them. Have children color and learn the message. Instruct them to take poster home and hang in their room a few weeks, then place in their journal.

Review Testimony and Challenge (page 18) in Primary 4 manual.*

SCRIPTURE CHALLENGE: Do activity in class or at home.

THOUGHT TREAT: <u>Choose the Right Treat Tree</u>. Stick a tree branch in a base of clay or play dough and hang treats from the branches. Treat Ideas: Wrapped chewy candies, i.e., salt water taffy, caramels, or bubble gum. Tell children to choose a chewy treat, to help them remember to "chews" the right.

Lesson #6*	**EXAMPLE: I Will Be a Good Example** *(Ship Shape family goal chart)*

YOU'LL NEED: Copy of Scripture Challenge card (page 94) and goal chart (page 10) on colored cardstock paper for each child, scissors, glue, and crayons.

ACTIVITY: Tell the story of Heavenly Father commanding Nephi to build a ship (1 Nephi 17) and give children this ship-shape goal chart to be a good example for their family.

Review Enrichment Activity #4 (page 20) and Testimony (page 21) in Primary 4 manual.*

1. Color chart.
2. Take chart home and place and "X" in the square when you have Family Home Evening, an "X" for each day you have family prayer, and an "X" for each day you have family scripture study.
3. Help children memorize 1 Nephi 17:15 (on the chart).

SCRIPTURE CHALLENGE: Do activity in class or at home.

THOUGHT TREAT: <u>Peanut Butter Banana Boat</u>. Cut a peeled banana in half lengthwise and then cut in half crosswise. Dig out the center and fill with peanut butter. Tell children that they can keep their life ship-shape by following the teachings of Jesus.

2 Nephi 4:15-24

"I know in whom I have trusted"

Like Nephi, I know that Heavenly Father will guide me if I trust in Him.

*Lesson #7**	**HOLY GHOST: I Want to Be Worthy to Receive His Spirit**
	(Don't "Wave"r maze)

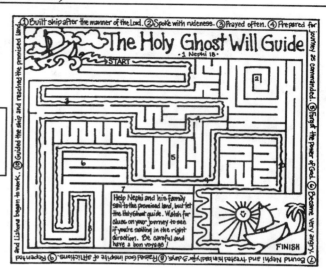

YOU'LL NEED: Copy of Scripture Challenge card (page 95) and Don't "Wave"r maze (page 12) on colored cardstock paper for each child, scissors, glue, and crayons.

ACTIVITY: Help children watch for clues to sail in the right direction, with the help of the Holy Ghost. Follow instructions and sail ahead to the promised land.

Review Enrichment Activity #3 (page 23) in Primary 4 manual.*

SCRIPTURE CHALLENGE: Do activity in class or at home.

THOUGHT TREAT: <u>Ahoy! Apple</u>. Core half an apple and fill with peanut butter. For the sail, place cheese slice on a toothpick.

*Lesson #8**	**TESTIMONY: My Testimony of Jesus**
	(What Would Jesus Do? Choice situation sack)

YOU'LL NEED: Copy of Scripture Challenge card (page 95) and choice situations and bag label (page 13) on colored cardstock paper, a zip-close plastic sandwich bag or small lunch sack, and peppermint candies (to place in bag) for each child, scissors, glue, pencils, and crayons.

ACTIVITY: Help children make choices in advance to give them power to withstand evil influences. Ask them to choose what Jesus would do when temptation comes.

Review Enrichment Activity #1 in Primary 4 manual.*

1. Color and cut out What Would Jesus Do? bag label to place inside a plastic bag or glue-mount on a paper bag.
2. Color and cut out choice situation cards and place inside bag.

SCRIPTURE CHALLENGE: Do activity in class or at home.

THOUGHT TREAT: <u>Starlight Mints</u>. Place 8 mints in each child's bag. Children can choose a situation from the bag while they eat their mint and think what Jesus would do in that situation.

The Holy Ghost Will Guide

·1 Nephi 18·

① Built ship after the manner of the Lord. ② Spoke with rudeness. ③ Prayed often. ④ Prepared for journey as commanded. ⑤ Forgot the power of God. ⑥ Became very angry. ⑦ Bound Nephi and treated him badly for 3 days. ⑧ Raised God in spite of afflictions. ⑨ Repented and Liahona began to work. ⑩ Guided the ship and reached the promised land.

START

FINISH

Help Nephi and his family sail to the promised land, but let the Holy Ghost guide. Watch for clues on your journey to see if you're sailing in the right direction. Be careful and — bon voyage! —

When someone asks me to steal, I say, "No deal!"

When asked to taste beer or wine, I decline.

When temptation is near, I choose the right and be of good cheer.

I pay my tenth before my money is spent.

When T.V. has a bad show, I turn it off and go!

Telling lies is so uncouth. Always tell the truth!

Bad words from me will not be heard.

If someone wants to pick a fight, turn and quickly get out of sight!

My testimony of Jesus Christ helps me make right choices. "Jesus mint" for me to be happy. So I must follow him.

What would Jesus do?

Lesson #9*	**PRAYER: I Can Pray for Blessings**
	(prayer plaque)

YOU'LL NEED: Copy of Scripture Challenge card (page 96) and prayer plaque (page 15) on colored cardstock paper for each guest, scissors, yarn or ribbon, glue, and crayons.

ACTIVITY: To encourage children to pray, create a tent-shaped prayer plaque to sit beside their bed. This reminder will motivate children to say their prayers.
1. Color and cut out prayer plaque.
2. Fold into diamond tent shape and insert tab where indicated.

Review Enrichment Activity #2 (page 30) in Primary 4 manual.*

SCRIPTURE CHALLENGE: Do activity in class or at home.

THOUGHT TREAT: Cloud 9 Prayer Pudding. Top pudding with whipped cream. Talk to children about that "cloud 9" feeling of joy they can feel whenever they pray. Heaven will feel closer each time they pray.

Lesson #10*	**BAPTISMAL COVENANTS: I Will Follow Jesus**
	(Commitment Connection rhyme and reason)

YOU'LL NEED: Copy of Scripture Challenge card (page 96) and Commitment Connection word find (page 16) on colored cardstock paper for each child, scissors, pencils, glue, and crayons.

ACTIVITY: Children can strengthen their commitment to keep their baptismal covenants by completing this Commitment Connection rhyme and reason word find.
1. Color the pictures in each box.
2. Fill in the missing word that rhymes with the picture in the corresponding box.

Review Enrichment Activity #1 (page 33) in Primary 4 manual.*

SCRIPTURE CHALLENGE: Do activity in class or at home.

I "CHEWS" TO BE BAPTIZED.
Why Is Eight Great?
Reason #1: I can be baptized at <u>eight</u> and make a commitment to obey Heavenly Father's commandments.
Reason #2: I can commit to living the Gospel of Jesus Christ in <u>eight</u> ways (review the Commitment Connection chart).
I can chew one of these 8 bubble gum balls each day and think of a baptism commitment.

THOUGHT TREAT: 8 Bubble Gum Balls. Place 8 bubble gum balls inside a plastic bag with a note (copy note on right). Read note with children.

Place this prayer plaque by your bed,
to remind you there's a prayer to be said.
Count your blessings one by one,
Thank Heavenly Father for all He's done.
Ask for blessings of your choice,
and listen to the still small voice.

Place this prayer plaque by your bed,
to remind you there's a prayer to be said.
Count your blessings one by one,
Thank Heavenly Father for all He's done.
Ask for blessings of your choice,
and listen to the still small voice.

Rhyme & Reason Word Find

COMMITMENT

CONNECTION

🗡	Have faith in the _____.
⛺	Re _____.
🛏	_____ the commandments.
👂	Be _____ to others.
🌙⭐	Don't _____ or quarrel.
🍽	_____ others.
🔔	Live the gos_____.

Fill in the missing word that rhymes with the picture in the box!

Lesson #11*	**MISSIONARY:** I Will Be Valiant and Tell Others About Jesus
	(Who is Abinadi? Prophet poster)

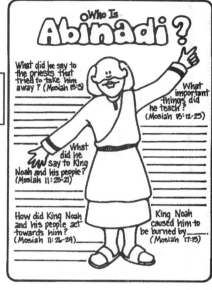

YOU'LL NEED: Copy of Scripture Challenge card (page 97) and prophet poster (page 18) on colored cardstock paper for each child, scissors, pencils, glue, and crayons.

ACTIVITY: Help children follow the prophet Abinadi, who was valiant in standing as a witness of Jesus Christ. Children can do the following:

Review Discussion and Application Questions (page 36) in Primary 4 manual*.

1. Look up scriptures to find the answers to each question.
2. Write in their own words the answer to each question.

SCRIPTURE CHALLENGE: Do activity in class or at home.

THOUGHT TREAT: Giant Prophet Cookie. Make gingerbread men cookies and decorate them to look like Abinadi. Talk about ways Abinadi was a giant of a man in spirit, i.e., boldly testifying to the wicked King Noah and his priests about the commandments (Mosiah 12:33-36 and Mosiah 13:11-24).

Lesson #12*	**BAPTISM:** I Will Keep My Baptismal Covenants
	(Waters of Mormon wordsearch)

YOU'LL NEED: Copy of Scripture Challenge card (page 97) and wordsearch (page 19) on cardstock paper for each child, scissors, glue, pencils, and crayons.

ACTIVITY: Follow Alma as he leads the righteous people away from the wicked King Noah. Help Alma lead them to the Waters of Mormon where they

Review Discussion and Application Questions (page 40) in Primary 4 manual*.

can be baptized into Jesus Christ's church. Complete the scripture word search to get there. Then color in the Waters of Mormon. **TO DO WORD SEARCH:** Search the scriptures to find the missing words. Circle the missing words in the Waters of Mormon.

SCRIPTURE CHALLENGE: Do activity in class or at home.

THOUGHT TREAT: Blueberry Punch. Drink blue punch and talk about the blue sky reflecting its blue color onto the Waters of Mormon as Alma baptized the saints.

Who Is Abinadi?

What did he say to the priests that tried to take him away? (Mosiah 13:3)
_____
_____
_____
_____

What important things did he teach? (Mosiah 13:12-25)
_____
_____
_____
_____
_____
_____

What did he say to King Noah and his people? (Mosiah 11:20-21)
_____
_____
_____

How did King Noah and his people act towards him? (Mosiah 11:26-29)
_____
_____
_____

King Noah caused him to be burned by _____. (Mosiah 17:15)

WATERS of MORMON
WORD SEARCH

Search the scriptures to find the missing words then circle the word in the word search below. Words go down, across or diagonal!

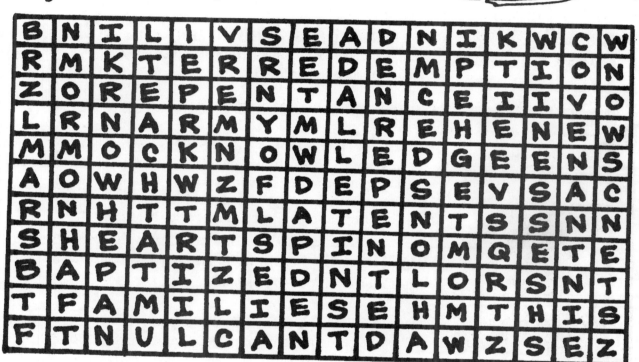

B	N	I	L	I	V	S	E	A	D	N	I	K	W	C	W
R	M	K	T	E	R	R	E	D	E	M	P	T	I	O	N
Z	O	R	E	P	E	N	T	A	N	C	E	I	I	V	O
L	R	N	A	R	M	Y	M	L	R	E	H	E	N	E	W
M	M	O	C	K	N	O	W	L	E	D	G	E	E	N	S
A	O	W	H	W	Z	F	D	E	P	S	E	V	S	A	C
R	N	H	T	T	M	L	A	T	E	N	T	S	S	N	N
S	H	E	A	R	T	S	P	I	N	O	M	Q	E	T	E
B	A	P	T	I	Z	E	D	N	T	L	O	R	S	N	T
T	F	A	M	I	L	I	E	S	E	H	M	T	H	I	S
F	T	N	U	L	C	A	N	T	D	A	W	Z	S	E	Z

① Alma _____ of his sins (Mosiah 18:1).   ② Alma did _____ the people about Jesus Christ (Mosiah 18:3).   ③ Alma preached _____ and _____ and _____ on the Lord (Mosiah 18:7).
④ Alma asked people to stand as _____ of God (Mosiah 8:9).
⑤ Desire in your _____ to be _____ and enter into a _____ (Mosiah 18:10).   ⑥ All this was done in the Waters of _____ (Mosiah 18:30).   ⑦ The people who were there came to a _____ of their Redeemer (Mosiah 18:30).   ⑧ The King sent his _____ to destroy them (Mosiah 18:33).   ⑨ They took their _____ and their _____ and departed into the wilderness (Mosiah 18:34).

ADVERSITY: My Faith in Jesus Christ will Help Me

Lesson #13*

(Times of Adversity lightswitch cover)

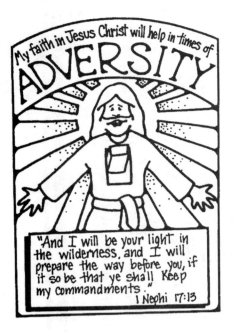

YOU'LL NEED: Copy of Scripture Challenge card (page 98) and lightswitch cover (page 21) on colored cardstock paper for each child, scissors, glue, and crayons.

ACTIVITY: Help children know they can be like King Limhi and his people and Alma and his people, who received help from Jesus Christ as they kept the commandments and asked for his help (Mosiah 21:31 and Mosiah 23:22).

Review Enrichment Activity #1 (page 46) in Primary 4 manual*.

TO MAKE LIGHTSWITCH COVER: Color and cut out. We can face the adversities by praying to our Father in Heaven with faith and humility (read 1 Nephi 17:13).

SCRIPTURE CHALLENGE: Do activity in class or at home.

THOUGHT TREAT: Frown and Smile Sandwich. Top your favorite sandwich with a cheesy frown and smile to show that in times of adversity you can smile, knowing that Jesus will light the way. Decorate sandwich using processed cheese from the can or tube, or cut out a face from a square piece of cheese or bologna.

REPENTANCE: I Can Live in Heaven

Lesson #14*

(Alma the Younger's Road to Repentance maze)

YOU'LL NEED: Copy of Scripture Challenge card (page 98) and repentance maze (page 22) on colored cardstock paper for each child, pencils, glue, and crayons.

ACTIVITY: Help children get through the maze, to remind children that repentance is necessary for earthly happiness and eternal life.

Review Scripture Account (pages 47-48) in Primary 4 manual*.

HOW TO GET THROUGH MAZE: Alma the Younger chose the wrong path. Help him get back on. Read the choice and choose for yourself the direction to go in order to repent and choose the righteous path.

SCRIPTURE CHALLENGE: Do activity in class or at home.

THOUGHT TREAT: Smile Sandwich. Make miniature sandwiches and decorate with a cheese smile from a cheese pressurized tube or can. Tell children that when we repent we become happy.

My faith in Jesus Christ will help in times of ADVERSITY

Cut Out

"And I will be your light in the wilderness, and I will prepare the way before you, if it so be that ye shall Keep my commandments." I Nephi 17:13

My faith in Jesus Christ will help in times of ADVERSITY

Cut Out

"And I will be your light in the wilderness, and I will prepare the way before you, if it so be that ye shall Keep my commandments." I Nephi 17:13

ALMA the YOUNGER

Road to Repentance Maze

Left? Right? Down? Up?

Alma the Younger chose the wrong path. Help him get back on. Follow the arrows and move the number of spaces shown, but if there are two arrows choose carefully to avoid the wrong path!

1 ↓	3 ...→ ↓	←...2 1 ↓	←...1	3 ↓	←...4
1 ...→	PERSECUTES OTHERS go back to start	1 ↓	1 ↑ ...→ REPENTS	1 ↑ 4 ↓	FINISH!
2 ↑ DOES NOT OBEY	←...1	2 ...→ LED BY THE SPIRIT	2 ...→	CONVERTS MANY 2 ↓	3 ↓
3 ...→ 1 ↓	1 ↑ ...→	2 ↓	CHANGE OF ♡ 2 ↑↓	1 ...→	3 ↑ 2 ↓
1 ...→	2 ↑	LIES go back to start	3 ↑ ↓ 1	1 ...→ LOVES OTHERS	3 ↑
2 ↑ START!	5 ↑	1 ↑	←...2 ...→	1 ...→ ↑ 2	2 ↑ ←...1

Lesson #15*	**OBEDIENCE:** I Will Obey Heavenly Father Like Alma and Amulek
	(missionary flip story)

YOU'LL NEED: Copy of Scripture Challenge card (page 99) and flip story pictures (pages 24) on colored cardstock paper, and flip story cue cards #1-6 (page 25) on lightweight paper for each child, scissors, glue, paper punch, string, tape, and crayons. OPTION: Page reinforcements (see #3 below).

AGES 8-TEEN ACTIVITY: Help children learn the importance of faithfully obeying Heavenly Father's commandments. Create a flip story to show how Alma and Amulek obeyed Heavenly Father and served their

Review Scripture Account: Alma 8:8–9:34 and 11:21–12:19 (page 51) in Primary 4 manual.*

mission. **TO MAKE FLIP STORY:** (1) Color and cut out picture cards #1-6. Cut out cue cards #1-6. (2) Glue cue cards #1-6 on backs of picture cards. Be sure to start gluing cue card #1 on the back of picture #6 (<u>don't</u> cut instructions off cue cards). (3) Tape over holes before punching holes, or punch holes and use page reinforcements. (4) Place string loosely through holes to make a flip chart.

SCRIPTURE CHALLENGE: Do activity in class or at home.

THOUGHT TREAT: Big "O" Doughnut to remind children to "O"bey.

Lesson #16*	**FAITH:** I Will Stand for the Right Like Alma and Amulek
	(persecution flip story)

YOU'LL NEED: Copy of Scripture Challenge card (page 99) and flip story pictures (page 26) on cardstock paper, and flip story cue cards #1-6 (page 27) on lightweight paper for each child, scissors, glue, tape, paper punch, string, and crayons. OPTION: Page reinforcements (see #3 below).

ACTIVITY: Help children develop faith in Jesus Christ so they can stand for the right. Create a flip story to show how Alma and Amulek made a commitment to

Review Scripture Account: Alma 14:1–16:10 (page 53) in Primary 4 manual.*

stand for right. **TO MAKE FLIP STORY:** (1) Color and cut out picture cards #1-6. Cut out cue cards #1-6. (2) Glue cue cards #1-6 on backs of picture cards. Be sure to start by gluing cue card #1 on the back of picture #6. <u>Don't</u> cut instructions off cue cards. (3) Tape over holes before punching holes, or punch holes and use page reinforcements. (4) Place string loosely through holes and tie.

SCRIPTURE CHALLENGE: Do activity in class or at home.

THOUGHT TREAT: <u>Sunflower Seeds</u>. Help children "plant" these seeds in their mouth as you say: "Plant the seeds of faith every day by reading the scriptures and following Jesus."

PATTERN: *OBEDIENCE (missionary flip story)*

PATTERN: *OBEDIENCE (missionary flip story)*

I Will Obey Heavenly Father

Alma the Younger was chosen by God to lead the church. He went out to teach the people to obey God's commandments. The people from some cities repented, were baptized, and started to obey God's commandments.

CUE CARD #1 - Glue to back of picture card #6

But the people from Ammonihah would not listen. In Alma 8:9 we learn that Satan had gotten hold upon the hearts of the people in Ammonihah. They would not listen. They forced Alma to leave.

CUE CARD #2 - Glue to back of picture card #1

Alma the Younger felt sorrow for the people. An angel came to him saying, "Alma ... lift up thy head and rejoice ... for thou hast been faithful in keeping the commandments of God." The angel commanded him to return to Ammonihah to preach to the people, to tell them to repent, or they would be destroyed.

CUE CARD #3 - Glue to back of picture card #2

Alma the Younger went back to Ammonihah and met a righteous man named Amulek who gave him food. Amulek went with Alma the Younger and told the people to repent.

CUE CARD #4 - Glue to back of picture card #3

Zeezrom, a wicked man, tried to trick Amulek into saying something that was not true. But Alma and Amulek were filled with the Spirit and knew the thoughts and intents of his heart. Zeezrom knew he was wrong and asked Alma and Amulek to teach him.

CUE CARD #5 - Glue to back of picture card #4

Alma the Younger obeyed Heavenly Father in teaching the people. He shared his testimony with them.
I, too, can obey Heavenly Father and tell others about the gospel of Jesus Christ.

CUE CARD #6 - Glue to back of picture card #5

PATTERN: *FAITH (persecution flip story)*

PATTERN: *FAITH (persecution flip story)*

I Will Stand for Right

God chose Alma the Younger to be the leader of the church. He loved the people and wanted them to be righteous. He felt sad when he saw that some of the people were wicked. Alma wanted to teach the people to obey God's commandments.

CUE CARD #1 - Glue to back of picture card #6

An angel told Alma the Younger to go back to the city of Ammonihah to tell the people to repent or they would be destroyed. In that city, Zeezrom was trying to blind the minds of the people with wickedness. Zeezrom listened, repented, and asked Alma the Younger and Amulek to teach him.

CUE CARD #2 - Glue to back of picture card #1

The wicked people in Ammonihah threw the righteous women and children into a pit of fire because they believed in Jesus Christ. The Holy Ghost told Alma the Younger to stand back, that the Lord would receive them into heaven. The people who were thrown into the fire would enter into the kingdom of God.

CUE CARD #3 - Glue to back of picture card #2

Alma the Younger and Amulek were thrown into prison. They were not given food and water, and they were beaten. They prayed and God helped them break the ropes. The earth shook and the prison walls fell. They walked out of prison, and the people of Ammonihah were afraid of them.

CUE CARD #4 - Glue to back of picture card #3

Alma the Younger and Amulek left Ammonihah to go to the city of Sidom. Many people in this city believed them. Zeezrom was there and felt sorry for the wicked things he had done. Alma the Younger and Amulek found him sick and blessed him. Zeezrom was healed and was baptized by Alma the Younger.

CUE CARD #5 - Glue to back of picture card #4

Zeezrom went to teach the people the gospel of Jesus Christ. Alma the Younger and Amulek baptized many and chose many leaders and teachers for Christ's church. I, too, will stand for the right and follow Jesus like Alma the Younger and Amulek.

CUE CARD #6 - Glue to back of picture card #5

Lesson #17*

MISSIONARY: I Will Share My Testimony of Jesus Christ
(name tag and testimony writing)

YOU'LL NEED: Copy of Scripture Challenge card (page 100) and name tag and My Testimony page (page 29) on colored cardstock for each child, scissors, pencils, glue, and crayons.

ACTIVITY: Encourage children to share the gospel of Jesus Christ by wearing home a missionary name tag and writing a testimony letter. (1) Color and cut out name tag and have children write their name on the tag. (2) Color and cut out the testimony page. (3) Have children write their personal testimony on the page. (4) Children can place their testimony in their own Book of Mormon or in one they plan to give away.

Review Enrichment Activity #2 (page 58) in Primary 4 manual.*

TESTIMONY IDEAS: Share your testimony of the Book of Mormon or of the Book of Mormon story Ammon the Great Servant (shown on the testimony letter -- See Alma 17:19-25, 18:8-40). Be sure to pray to see if the story and the Book of Mormon are true as Moroni suggested in Moroni 10:4 (the Book of Mormon promise). You can even suggest this scripture in your testimony writing.

SCRIPTURE CHALLENGE: Do activity in class or at home.

THOUGHT TREAT: <u>Licorice Links</u>. Create a licorice chain with strings of red or black licorice by tying licorice strings into loops or knots to make a chain. Remind children that every part of the gospel of Jesus Christ is important to build a strong testimony. Each part connects to a long chain of happiness. Sharing the gospel links us all together. When one believes because of missionary work, there is another link in the chain.

Lesson #18*

FORGIVENESS: Plan for Redemption
(King Lamoni's father scripture story)

YOU'LL NEED: Copy of Scripture Challenge card (page 100) and scripture story (page 30) on colored cardstock paper for each child, scissors, pencils, glue, and crayons.

ACTIVITY: Encourage children to find out how Ammon converted King Lamoni's father. (1) Read scriptures #1-6 at the top. (2) Place the numbers 1-6 in right order in the boxes below to create a scripture story. (3) Color the pictures and read the story in order of #1-6.

Review Scripture Account (page 61) in Primary 4 manual.*

SCRIPTURE CHALLENGE: Do activity in class or at home.

THOUGHT TREAT: <u>Hope-ful Cupcakes</u>. Write the reference Alma 22:14 on strip of paper, wrap in aluminum foil, and place inside ready-baked cupcakes. As children find the message, have them look up the scripture to read aloud together. NOTE: Have wet-wipes or a wet cloth ready to wash their hands before touching their scriptures. Talk about the scripture and the <u>hope</u> we have because of Jesus.

PATTERN: *MISSIONARY (name tag and testimony writing)*

Conversion of King Lamoni's Father

1. Alma 20:1-5   **2.** Alma 20:10, 13-14   **3.** Alma 20:26-27
4. Alma 22:1, 4-5   **5.** Alma 22:6   **6.** Alma 22:12

After Ammon converted King Lamoni to the gospel of Jesus Christ, he began teaching his people continually. Meanwhile, Aaron, one of Ammon's brethren, was led by the Spirit to the land of Nephi to teach King Lamoni's father. King Lamoni's father was troubled about the Spirit of the Lord.

Scripture

Along the way they met King Lamoni's father, who was king over all the Lamanites. King Lamoni's father thought Ammon was a liar and a robber. He did not trust him. He wanted Lamoni to kill him with his sword.

Scripture

King Lamoni's father said to Aaron, "What is this that Ammon said -- If ye repent ye shall be saved, and if ye will not repent, ye shall be cast off at the last day?"

Scripture

LET'S CONVERT THIS STORY ABOUT A CONVERSION:

Help tell the story of how Ammon and Aaron converted King Lamoni's father to the gospel of Jesus Christ. King Lamoni's father was king over all the Lamanites.

Learn the order of the scripture story by doing the following:
1. Read scriptures #1-6.
2. Place the scriptures in the right order by writing the reference below the story section and the corresponding number in the square.
3. Color the picture and tell the story in order.

When Aaron could see that King Lamoni's father would believe his words, "he began from the creation of Adam, reading the scriptures unto the king--how God created man after his own image, and that God gave him commandments, and that because of transgression, man had fallen." He told about the plan of redemption whereby we may be forgiven of our sins. The king and all his household were converted.

Scripture

King Lamoni wanted to take Ammon to the land of Nephi to preach the gospel. God told Ammon not to go to Nephi as his life was in danger. God told Ammon to go to Middoni instead, to deliver Aaron and his other brethren who were in prison. King Lamoni said he would go with him to talk to the king of the land.

Scripture

King Lamoni's father saw the love his son had for Ammon. His heart was softened, and he allowed Ammon to go to Middoni to release his brethren from prison.

Scripture

Lesson #19*	**COVENANTS: I Will Keep Sacred Covenants**
	(Weapons of War Buried for Peace pop-up quiz)

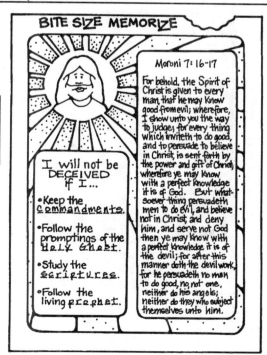

YOU'LL NEED: Copy of Scripture Challenge card (page 101) and sword (pages 32-33) on colored cardstock paper for each child, scissors, pencils, glue, and crayons.

ACTIVITY: Learn about the Anti-Nephi-Lehies to strengthen each child's desire to keep sacred covenants. Create a sword with a pop-out quiz to review why the weapons of war were buried for peace.

Review Scripture Account (page 65) in Primary 4 manual*.

1. Color and cut out sword and sword holder.
2. Fold sword and glue.
3. Fold sword holder and glue edges only, leaving top open for sword.
4. Answer the questions to the quiz on the back of sword.
5. Pop sword into holder to save as a reminder.

SCRIPTURE CHALLENGE: Do activity in class or at home.

THOUGHT TREAT: Sword Breadsticks. Cut strips of ready-made unbaked bread dough into sword shapes and twist dough at the top to make handle and bake at 350° for 20-25 minutes. Remind children that those who buried their swords had a firm testimony of Jesus Christ, and they did not want to sin or kill others with their swords.

Lesson #20*	**TRUTH: I Can Know the Truth and Follow Jesus**
	(bite-size memorize Moroni 7:16-17)

YOU'LL NEED: Copy of Scripture Challenge card (page 101) and bite-size memorize poster (page 34) on colored cardstock paper for each child, scissors, glue, and crayons.

ACTIVITY: Encourage children to memorize Moroni 7:16-17 to be able to judge good from evil, to avoid temptation and follow Jesus.

Review Enrichment Activity #1 (page 68) in Primary 4 manual*.

SCRIPTURE CHALLENGE: Do activity in class or at home.

THOUGHT TREAT: Truthful Treats. Plan a variety of treats that children can taste like a tasting table. Have children taste these treats and tell the truth. Do they like them or not? To trick their taste-buds, put a few sour or salty items along with sweet things.

BITE SIZE MEMORIZE

I will not be DECEIVED if I...
- Keep the commandments.
- Follow the promptings of the Holy Ghost.
- Study the scriptures.
- Follow the living prophet.

Moroni 7: 16-17

For behold, the Spirit of Christ is given to every man that he may know good from evil; wherefore, I show unto you the way to judge; for every thing which inviteth to do good, and to persuade to believe in Christ, is sent forth by the power and gift of Christ; wherefore ye may know with a perfect knowledge it is of God. But whatsoever thing persuadeth men to do evil, and believe not in Christ, and deny him, and serve not God then ye may know with a perfect knowledge it is of the devil; for after this manner doth the devil work, for he persuadeth no man to do good, no, not one, neither do his angels; neither do they who subject themselves unto him.

*Primary 4 manual is published by The Church of Jesus Christ of Latter-day Saints, Salt Lake City, Utah.

31

PATTERN: *COVENANTS (Weapons of War Buried for Peace pop-up quiz)*

ANTI-NEPHI-LEHIES
Weapons of war buried for peace.

Let us _ _ _ _ them away that they may be kept _ _ _ _ _ _ as a _ _ _ _ _ _ _ _ _ to our God at the last _ _ _ _ .

Alma 24:15

PATTERN: *COVENANTS (Weapons of War Buried for Piece pop-up quiz)*

·· Answers ···· ·· Questions ···

Answers

<u>1.</u> The teachings of
_____ and his
brethren.

<u>2.</u> Anti-____-____.

<u>3.</u> To repent of
their ____ and
many ____.

<u>4.</u> Rather than shed
____ they
would give up their
own ____.

Questions

<u>1.</u> What brought the
Lamanites to a knowledge
of the truth? Alma 23:5-6

<u>2.</u> What new name did
the Lamanites want to
be called? Alma 23:16-17

<u>3.</u> Why were they never
to fight their enemies?
Alma 24:10-13,16

<u>4.</u> What covenant of
promise did they make?
Alma 24:17-18

BITE SIZE MEMORIZE

I will not be DECEIVED if I...

- Keep the
  _ _ _ _ _ _ _ _ _ _ _ _ _ _ _ _ _ _ _

- Follow the promptings of the
  _ _ _ _ _ _ _ _ _ _ _ _ _ _ _

- Study the
  _ _ _ _ _ _ _ _ _ _ _ _ _ _ _ _ _ _

- Follow the living _ _ _ _ _ _ _ _ _ _ _ _ _ _

Moroni 7: 16-17

For behold, the Spirit of Christ is given to every man, that he may know good from evil; wherefore, I show unto you the way to judge; for every thing which inviteth to do good, and to persuade to believe in Christ, is sent forth by the power and gift of Christ; wherefore ye may know with a perfect knowledge it is of God. But whatsoever thing persuadeth men to do evil, and believe not in Christ, and deny him, and serve not God then ye may know with a perfect knowledge it is of the devil; for after this manner doth the devil work, for he persuadeth no man to do good, no, not one, neither do his angels; neither do they who subject themselves unto him.

Lesson #21*	**WORSHIP: I Can Be Humble and Help** *(Pocket-full of Humble Deeds secret service)*

YOU'LL NEED: Copy of Scripture Challenge card (page 102) and Secret Service pocket, list, and buttons (page 36) on colored cardstock paper for each child, scissors, glue, and crayons.

ACTIVITY: Help children realize the importance of doing good deeds in a humble, quiet manner, not like the Zoramites, who boasted and were full of pride (Alma 31:15-17, 20).

> *Review Enrichment Activity #2 (page 72) in Primary 4 manual*.*

1. Color and cut out pocket, list, and secret service buttons.
2. Fold pocket and glue sides and bottom, leaving top open.
3. Encourage children to add Secret Service Deeds by writing on the back of list. Insert list and buttons in pocket.

SECRET SERVICE DEEDS: Read the scripture Alma 34:28-29 and encourage children to take their pocket full of humble deeds home and secretly leave one wherever they do a good deed.

SCRIPTURE CHALLENGE: Do activity in class or at home.

THOUGHT TREAT: Red-Hot Candy Hearts. Add a few red-hot candy hearts to their Secret Service pocket full of secret service buttons. Tell children that each time they do a loving service, they can eat a Red-Hot Candy Heart to remind them of the service rendered.

Lesson #22*	**FAITH: I Will Plant and Grow Seeds of Faith** *(growing tree flip book)*

YOU'LL NEED: Copy of Scripture Challenge card (page 102) and faith flip book (pages 37-40) on colored lightweight paper for each child, scissors, stapler, glue, and crayons.

ACTIVITY: Create a faith flip book (a tree that starts small and grows into a large tree as you flip the pages). Talk about Alma's teachings on faith (Alma 32-33). Compare this growing tree to the word of God that grows when we

> *Review Attention Activity (page 74) in Primary 4 manual*.*

nourish it with faith. It will grow in our hearts, creating a testimony of Jesus Christ, but we must first plant the seeds and have faith that they will grow. (1) Color and cut out faith flip book pages. (2) Place smaller trees in front and larger in back. (3) Staple book together and flip pages to show how faith can grow in our hearts creating a testimony.

SCRIPTURE CHALLENGE: Do activity in class or at home.

THOUGHT TREAT: Apple Seeds of Faith. Divide an apple in half to show children the seeds that were planted in the ground to create a tree to grow this apple. Our own seeds of faith need to be planted every day if we are to keep our testimony tree growing.

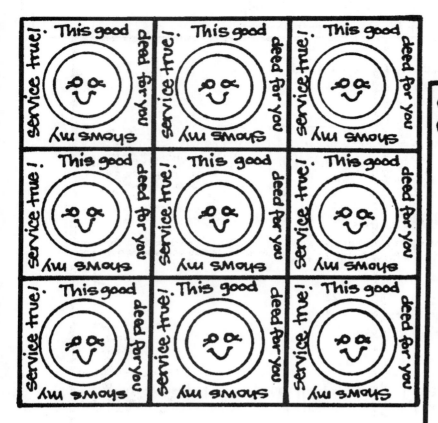

Secret Service Deeds

- Make someone's bed
- Wash windows
- Tend brothers & sisters
- Polish someone's shoes
- Sweep the porch
- Do the dishes
- Fold the clothes
- Make a treat
- Dust the whole house
- Rake the lawn
- Think of other things you can do!

A POCKET-FULL OF HUMBLE DEEDS

Service is a joy to do.
I show my love through service true!

SECRET SERVICE WEEK

Alma 34:28-29

Fold & glue

Fold & glue

Fold & glue

PATTERN: *FAITH (growing tree flip book)*

PATTERN: *FAITH (growing tree flip book)*

PATTERN: *FAITH (growing tree flip book)*

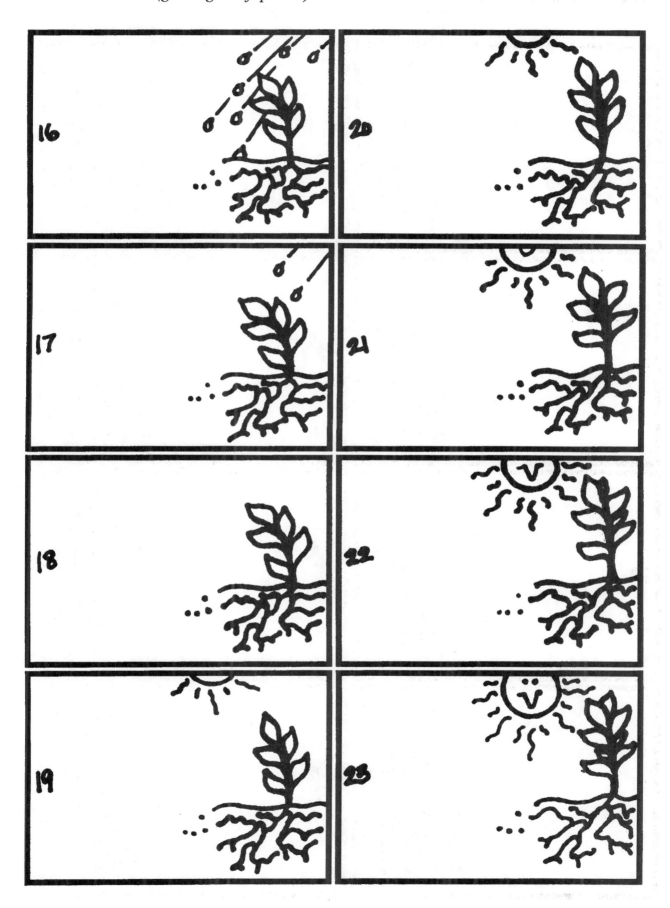

PATTERN: *FAITH (growing tree flip book)*

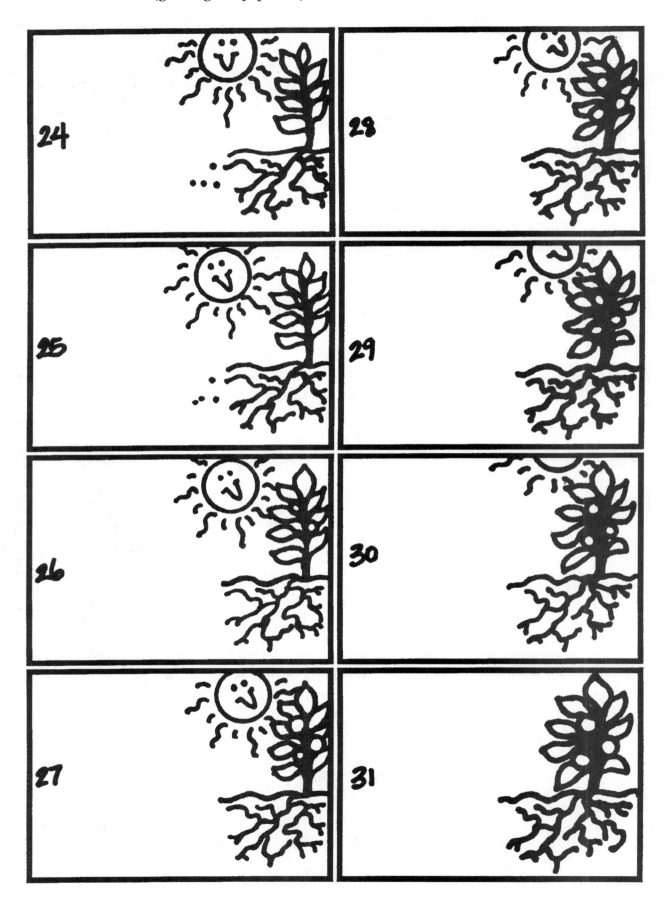

Lesson #23*	**SCRIPTURES** Guide Me to My Heavenly Home
	(Straight and Narrow Arrow scripture underlining ruler)

YOU'LL NEED: Copy of Scripture Challenge card (page 103) and scripture underlining ruler (page 42) on cardstock paper for each child, scissors, and crayons.

Straight & Narrow Arrow
The scriptures will guide me to my heavenly home!

ACTIVITY: Create a straight and narrow arrow scripture underlining ruler for each child to mark their scriptures and motivate scripture reading.

Help children find Alma 7:9 and underline the scripture:
"Repent ye, and prepare the way of the Lord, and walk in his paths, which are straight..."

Review Testimony (page 81) in Primary 4 manual.*

1. Color and cut out ruler.
2. Fold and glue back-to-back.
3. Laminate for durability using clear contact paper.

SCRIPTURE CHALLENGE: Do activity in class or at home.

THOUGHT TREAT: Ruler Wafer Cookie. Frost a wafer cookie with ruler markings.

Lesson #24*	**CHOICES:** I Will Be Happy as I Make Right Choices
	(Value-Pack book of good choices)

YOU'LL NEED: Copy of Scripture Challenge card (page 103) and Value-Pack book of good choices (pages 43-44) on colored cardstock paper and a 6" piece of yarn or ribbon for each child, scissors, paper punch, glue, and crayons.

ACTIVITY: Talk about the good and bad consequences that happen when we make good and bad choices. Create a Value-Pack book of good choices to help children record ways they can make good choices.

Review Enrichment Activity #2 (page 85) in Primary 4 manual.*

TO MAKE: (1) Color and cut out book of good values.
(2) Paper punch holes top left. (3) Tie 6" piece of yarn or ribbon at the top to hold book pages together.

SCRIPTURE CHALLENGE CARD: Assign each child a new card and reward them with a glue-on sticker for the card completed.

THOUGHT TREAT: Cherry Pie. Purchase small cherry pies at the bakery, cut in half and serve. Tell children the saying, "Life can be a bowl of cherries." If you make the right choices, life can be sweet and full of rich color. Blessings come from keeping a cheery disposition. A cheery disposition or happy face comes from feeling happy inside. This happy feeling comes from keeping the commandments.

PATTERN: *SCRIPTURES (Straight and Narrow Arrow scripture underlining ruler)*

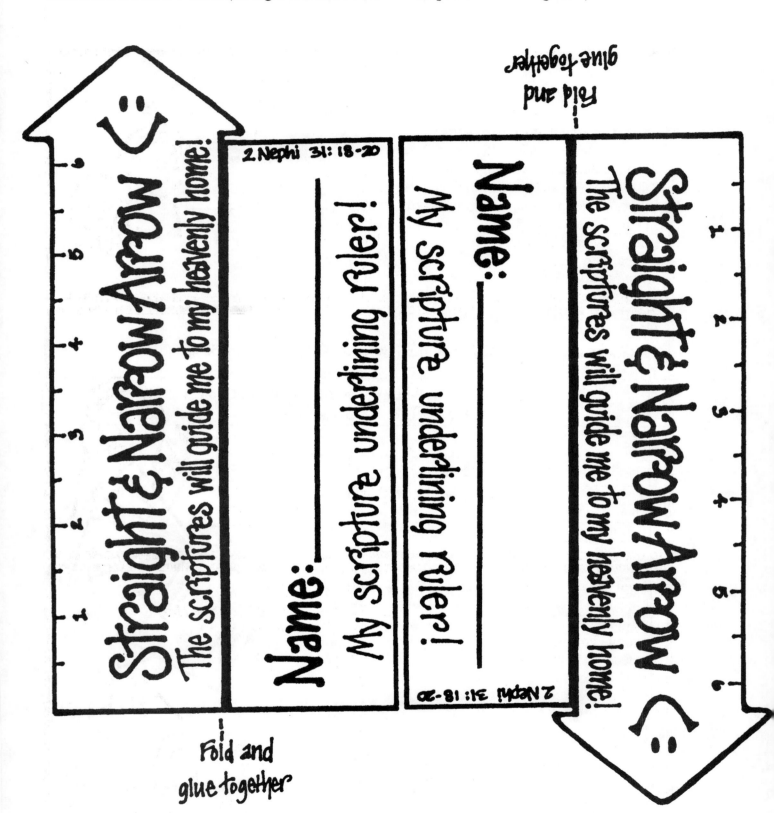

PATTERN: *CHOICES (Value-Pack book of good choices)*

☺

Value-Pack
of Good Choices:
The choices in this book
should not be overlooked.
Try one each day to see
what kind of person you will be.

**GOOD CONSEQUENCES
or good happenings**

☺ CHOICE #1
Be a Good Friend
CHALLENGE--I will
do the following to be
a good friend:

_____
_____
_____
_____

☺ CHOICE #2
Choose Good Language
CHALLENGE--I will
do the following to
watch my tongue
(language) while I am
young:

_____
_____
_____
_____

☺ CHOICE #3
Be Honest
CHALLENGE--I will
do the following to
give an honest
compliment:

_____
_____
_____
_____

☺ CHOICE #4
Be Modest & Clean
CHALLENGE--I will
do the following to
keep my body covered
and wear clean
clothes:

_____
_____
_____
_____

☺ CHOICE #5
Keep the Sabbath Day Holy
CHALLENGE--I will
do the following to
keep the Sabbath Day
Heavenly Father's
way:

_____
_____
_____
_____

PATTERN: *CHOICES (Value-Pack book of good choices)*

☺ CHOICE #6

Be a Good Son or Daughter
CHALLENGE--I will
do the following to
make Mom and Dad
be glad I'm me:

_____
_____
_____
_____

☺ CHOICE #7

Be a Seeker of Wholesome Entertainment
CHALLENGE--I will
do the following to
seek out fun things to
do that will invite the
Holy Spirit too:

_____
_____
_____
_____

☹ CHOICE #8

Allow Truth to Burn Bright
CHALLENGE--I will
do the following to
invite the light of truth
(Holy Ghost) into my
life:

_____
_____
_____
_____

☺ CHOICE #9

Read Good Magazines and Books
CHALLENGE--I will
do the following to
grow in knowledge
and wisdom:

_____
_____
_____
_____

☺ CHOICE #10

Music That Uplifts and Inspires
CHALLENGE--I will
do the following to
enjoy music that
brings me peace and
strength:

_____
_____
_____
_____

☺ CHOICE #11

Be Honest in All I Do and Say
CHALLENGE--I will
do the following to
leave things alone that
are not my own, and
speak only truth:

_____
_____
_____
_____

Lesson #25*	**ARMOR OF GOD Will Protect Me from Evil**
	(Fight for Right! word choice)

YOU'LL NEED: Copy of Scripture Challenge card (page 104) and Fight for Right! Word choice (page 46) on colored cardstock paper for each child, scissors, glue, pencils, and crayons.

ACTIVITY: Show children how they can Fight for Right! and follow Captain Moroni's example to put on the whole armor of God. Help them search for and black out wrong choices to see ways they can fight for right! Then have children color Captain Moroni.

Review Enrichment Activity #3 (page 87) in Primary 4 manual*.

SCRIPTURE CHALLENGE: Do activity in class or at home.

THOUGHT TREAT: Right-Hand Cookie. Roll out sugar cookie dough and cut out a right-hand print or right-hand mitten shape. Bake at 350° for 8-10 minutes. As children eat right-hand cookie hand, remind them to fight for right!

Lesson #26*	**FREEDOM: I Stand for Right and Resist Evil**
	(My Personal Title of Liberty)

YOU'LL NEED: Copy of liberty flag (page 47) and SCRIPTURE CHALLENGE CARD (page 104) on colored cardstock paper for each child, scissors, glue, pencils, crayons, and string or a wooden dowel

ACTIVITY: Help children create their own personal Title of Liberty to express what they are, what they hope to be, and what they stand for. Help them to know that freedom

Review Attention Activity (page 92) and Enrichment Activity #2 (page 94) in Primary 4 manual*.

comes from resisting evil and keeping Heavenly Father's commandments as Captain Moroni did.
1. Color and cut out My Personal Title of Liberty flag.
2. Draw a picture or write your personal plan to resist evil.
3. Hang flag on wall with string, or place flag on a wooden dowel to display as a banner.

SCRIPTURE CHALLENGE: Do activity in class or at home.

THOUGHT TREAT: Title of Liberty Freedom Flag. Make a flag by dividing a slice of processed cheese in half and placing a toothpick in the side for the flag pole). Tell children that the choices they make can make them free. Read about the Title of Liberty in Alma 46:12-13.

FIGHT FOR RIGHT

Follow CAPTAIN MORONI'S example:

Put on the whole armor of God

Black out wrong choices to see ways you can fight for right!

lazy	scriptures
pray	angry
~~temptation~~	service
church	cheat
tithing	friend
rude	swear
kind	honest
sad	steal
Kindness	complain
lie	happy
helpful	love
hit	gentle

My Personal

Title of Liberty

What I am, hope to be, and stand for......

I am free when I keep
the commandments.
Alma 46:12-13

Lesson #27*	**RIGHTEOUSNESS: I Will Honor My Parents** *(thank you card)*

YOU'LL NEED: Copy of Scripture Challenge card (page 105) and thank you card (page 49) on colored cardstock paper and legal envelope (option) for each child, scissors, pencils, glue, and crayons.

ACTIVITY: Help children learn ways they can honor their parents and defend truth and right like Helaman's two thousand warriors. Read Alma 56:47. Then, help them create a thank you card to give to their own parents or loved ones. (1) Color and cut out card. (2) Fan-fold card. (3) Glue first and second flaps back to back. (4) Place in a legal size envelope (option).

Review Scripture Account (page 96) in Primary 4 manual*.

SCRIPTURE CHALLENGE: Do activity in class or at home.

THOUGHT TREAT: Courage Chewing Gum. Write Alma 56:45 on strip of paper and glue it to the wrapper of a stick of chewing gum. Tell children that if they "chews" to have faith in Jesus Christ and "chews" the right, they will have the courage to defend truth and right.

Lesson #28*	**CHOOSE THE RIGHT: I Will Live the Teachings of Jesus** *(CTR Commitment Calendar)*

YOU'LL NEED: Copy of Scripture Challenge card (page 105) and CTR Commitment Calendar (pages 50-51) on colored cardstock paper for each child, scissors, glue, and crayons.

ACTIVITY: Help children build a sure foundation to build upon the rock which is Jesus Christ. Let each child create a CTR Commitment Calendar to look at each day Monday through Sunday to commit their lives to living the teachings of Jesus. (1) Color and cut out parts A, B,

Review Attention Activity (page 100) in Primary 4 manual*.

C, and D of calendar. (2) Glue together as shown above. (3) Write goals to help you remember to live the teachings of Jesus. (4) Encourage child to post calendar next to their bed or over bed headboard to remind them to choose the right each day.

SCRIPTURE CHALLENGE: Do activity in class or at home.

THOUGHT TREAT: CTR Breadsticks. Make a batch of bread dough or purchase ready-made bread stick dough in the freezer section at your grocer to make this fun reminder. Cut and curve bread stick dough into "C," and "T," and "R" shapes for each child. Bake at 350° for 20-25 minutes. Package each CTR Breadstick set in a zip-close plastic sandwich bag to give to each child. Tell them that Choosing The Right each day is just as important as the food you eat. Choosing The Right keeps your spirit healthy, just as eating good foods makes your body healthy and strong. We need to feed both our spirit and our body to take care of what Heavenly Father has given us.

PATTERN: *RIGHTEOUSNESS (thank you card)*

I am like the army of Helaman. I have been taught in my youth.

THANK YOU for your guidance!

Fold

Fold

MY CTR COMMIT

(A) Jesus is my rock.

MONDAY
I CHOOSE TO FOLLOW JESUS BY preparing Family Home Evening to help teach the gospel of Jesus Christ and to _____ together. Today I will do the following to get ready for Family Home Evening:

3 Nephi 18:21

ATTACH B HERE

MITMENT CALENDAR

(B)

TUESDAY
I CHOOSE TO FOLLOW JESUS BY getting my tithing ready to pay. If I do not want to _____ God. When I pay my tithing the _____ of heaven will be opened. This week I will pay this amount in tithing: _____

3 Nephi 24:8-10

WEDNESDAY
I CHOOSE TO FOLLOW JESUS BY studying the scriptures. I take upon myself the name of _____ to be called _____ that name in the last days. I belong to The Church of Jesus Christ of Latter-day Saints. The following is my schedule for reading the scriptures.
Days:
Times:

3 Nephi 27:5

ATTACH C HERE.

•I will study the scriptures each day.

C.

THURSDAY

2 Nephi 32:8

I CHOOSE TO FOLLOW JESUS BY praying about my problems. the Spirit of Truth teaches me that I must ——————— unto the Spirit. This means I will do what the Spirit tells me to do. This is what I will pray about:

FRIDAY

Helaman 5:11

I CHOOSE TO FOLLOW JESUS BY repenting of things I have done wrong. I can be happy as I repent of the following:

This is how I will do better: ——————

ATTACH D HERE

pray and live the righteous way!

D.

SATURDAY

Alma 41:3

I CHOOSE TO FOLLOW JESUS BY working hard and serving others to help prepare for the Sabbath Day. Then if work is done I will enjoy my play. This is what I will do to work:

This is what I will do to play: ——————

SUNDAY

Helaman 5:12

I CHOOSE TO FOLLOW JESUS BY going to church today. This way I can build a strong foundation. This is what I will do to build my testimony of Jesus Christ:

For Jesus is my rock!

Lesson #29*	**PROPHETS Guide Me** *(Prophet Nephi's Warnings scripture search)*

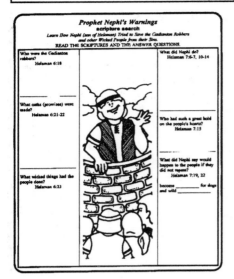

YOU'LL NEED: Copy of Scripture Challenge card (page 106) and scripture search (page 53) on colored cardstock paper for each child, pencils, and crayons.

ACTIVITY: Answer the questions in the scripture search boxes to learn of Nephi's warnings to the Gadianton robbers. Learn of this prophet's warnings to repent and have faith in the Savior. Know that wickedness can only bring destruction.

> *Review Scripture Account and Discussion (pages 103-104) in Primary 4 manual*.*

SCRIPTURE CHALLENGE: Do activity in class or at home.

THOUGHT TREAT: <u>Scripture Scroll Fruit Roll-up</u>. Purchase fruit roll-ups or fruit leather. As children unroll and eat the fruit leather, describe how in ancient days, the prophets kept records on scrolls (parchment paper and rolled on a stick). The prophets rolled them out to write on them and to read what was written on them.

Lesson #30*	**PRIESTHOOD: Special Power to Guide and Bless Us** *(Plug into Priesthood Power Lines)*

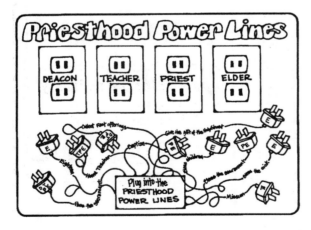

YOU'LL NEED: Copy of Scripture Challenge card (page 106) and Priesthood Power Lines activity (page 54) for each child, pens, and crayons.

ACTIVITY: Help children plug into Priesthood Power Lines by writing initials on the plug showing the duties, e.g. PE = Priest and Elder can bless the sacrament. Read Aaronic Priesthood duties (D&C 20:46-59) and Melchizedek Priesthood duties (D&C 20:38-45; 107:11-12).

> *Review Enrichment Activity #2 (page 108) in Primary 4 manual*.*

PRIESTHOOD DUTIES: ♥ A <u>DEACON</u>, at age 12, can hold the Aaronic Priesthood, pass the sacrament, act as a messenger for priesthood leaders, collect fast offerings, and care for church buildings and grounds.
♥ A <u>TEACHER</u>, at age 14, can hold the Aaronic Priesthood, perform all duties of a deacon, prepare bread and water for the sacrament, and be assigned to be a home teacher. ♥ A <u>PRIEST</u>, at age 16, can hold the Aaronic Priesthood, perform all duties of deacon and teacher, administer and bless the sacrament, and baptize. ♥ An <u>ELDER</u>, at age 18, can hold the Melchizedek Priesthood, may serve a full-time mission, watch over the Church, give the gift of the Holy Ghost, conduct meetings, bless children, administer to the sick, and bless family members.

SCRIPTURE CHALLENGE: Do activity in class or at home.

THOUGHT TREAT: <u>Priesthood Power Cookies</u>. Roll out sugar cookie dough and cut out a wall plug (see page 65). Write Deacon, Teacher, Priest, or Elder on cookies. As children eat the cookie, see if they can name the duties of the Priesthood named on their cookie.

Prophet Nephi's Warnings
scripture search
Learn How Nephi (son of Helaman) Tried to Save the Gadianton Robbers and other Wicked People from their Sins.
READ THE SCRIPTURES AND THE ANSWER QUESTIONS.

Who were the Gadianton robbers?
　　　　Helaman 6:18

_____

What oaths (promises) were made?
　　　　Helaman 6:21-22

_____

What wicked things had the people done?
　　　　Helaman 6:23

What did Nephi do?
　　　　Helaman 7:6-7, 10-14

_____

Who had such a great hold on the people's hearts?
　　　　Helaman 7:15

_____

What did Nephi say would happen to the people if they did not repent?
　　　　Helaman 7:19, 22

become _____ for dogs and wild _____

Lesson #31*	**PROPHETS Tell Me About the Life and Mission of Jesus** *(prophet poster presentation)*

YOU'LL NEED: Copy of Scripture Challenge card (page 107) and prophet posters and cue cards (pages 56-57) on colored cardstock paper for each child, scissors, glue, and crayons.

ACTIVITY: Help children create a prophet poster presentation showing Alma, Samuel the Lamanite, Nephi, and Abinadi telling the people of the life and mission of Jesus Christ. (1) Color and cut out poster and matching cue card. (2) Glue matching cue card to back of poster. (3) Show poster and read cue card.

Review Attention Activity and Scripture Account and Discussion (pages 111-112) in Primary 4 manual.*

SCRIPTURE CHALLENGE: Do activity in class or at home.

THOUGHT TREAT: Christmas Celebration Cake. Make a birthday cake to celebrate the birth of Jesus with a star on top. Tell children that people were told Jesus would come and be their Savior. When he finally did come, it was a great celebration!

Lesson #32*	**SIGNS Can Strengthen My Testimony of Jesus** *(Sign Seeker show-and-tell)*

YOU'LL NEED: Copy of Scripture Challenge card (page 107) and posters and cue cards (pages 58-60) on colored cardstock paper for each child, scissors, glue, and crayons.

ACTIVITY: Create a Sign Seeker show-and-tell to tell of Laman and Lemuel who saw an angel, Sherem who was smitten of God, and Korihor who was struck dumb. The stories tell how testimonies were changed when a sign was given. A sign is an event that shows the power of God. (1) Color and cut out poster and matching cue card. (2) Glue matching cue card to back of poster. (3) Show poster and read cue card and suggested scripture.

Review Discussion (pages 114-115) and Enrichment Activity #1 (page 115) in Primary 4 manual.*

SCRIPTURE CHALLENGE: Do activity in class or at home.

THOUGHT TREAT: Star Cookie. Follow sugar cookie recipe and make star shapes, then frost with yellow frosting. Explain to children that sometimes signs are given to show the wicked the power of God or strengthen the testimonies of the faithful. The star on the night of Jesus' birth was a sign to the wise men.

PATTERN: *PROPHETS (prophet poster presentation)*

Samuel the Lamanite prophet on a city wall told the people that Jesus would come in 5 years. He said a sign would come—great lights would be in heaven. And in the night before he was born there would be no darkness; it would be like day. The day of his birth a new star would appear. Helaman 14:2-6

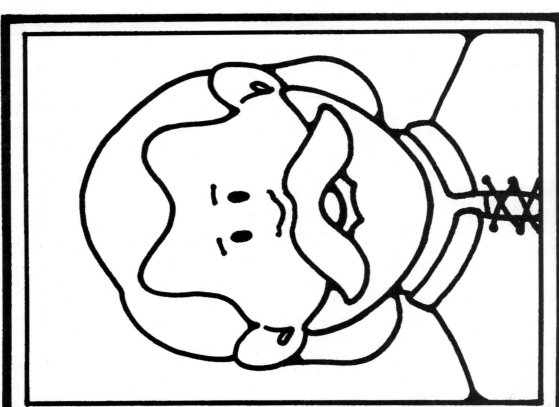

The Nephite prophet **Alma** had a vision of Jesus about 100 years before he came. He saw that Jesus would be born of Mary in Jerusalem. He would suffer pains and afflictions and temptations of every kind that we might be saved. He would loose the bands of death for everyone. Alma 7:10-12

PATTERN: *PROPHETS (prophet poster presentation)*

The prophet Nephi the son of Lehi lived 600 years before Jesus. He told of his vision, seeing the virgin, the mother of the Son of God bearing a child in her arms.
1 Nephi 11:20-22

The prophet Abinadi lived 150 years before Jesus. Abinadi told the people that "God himself shall come down among the children of men, and shall redeem his people ... (breaking) the bands of death, (taking) upon himself their iniquity (sins)...."
Mosiah 15:1; 7, 9

PATTERN: *SIGNS (Sign Seeker show-and-tell)*

 **Laman and Lamuel** were sons of Lehi. They lived 600 years B.C. (Before Jesus was born). They traveled with their brother Nephi and their family in the wilderness. They lacked faith, murmured against their father, and asked for a sign. **WHAT SIGN DID LAMAN AND LAMUEL SEEK AND RECEIVE?**
Let's read: 1 Nephi 3:28-31 and 1 Nephi 17:45

PATTERN: *SIGNS (Sign Seeker show-and-tell)*

 **Sherem** denied Christ. He argued with Jacob, the brother of Nephi.
He demanded that Jacob show him a sign. What happened to
Sherem? **WHAT SIGN DID SHEREM SEEK AND RECEIVE?**
Let's read: Jacob 7:13-20.

PATTERN: *SIGNS (Sign Seeker show-and-tell)*

Korihor taught the people that there was no God or no punishment for sin. He preached against Christ. He led many people into wickedness. He tried to preach this wickedness to the people of Ammon. The people rejected his teachings and took him to Ammon, the high priest. Korihor asked Alma to show him a sign to prove that there is a God. **WHAT SIGN DID KORIHOR SEEK AND RECEIVE?** Let's read: Alma 30:43-56

Lesson #33*	**TESTIMONY: I Have a Testimony of Jesus Christ** *(love and gratitude journal)*

YOU'LL NEED: Copy of Scripture Challenge card (page 108) and love and gratitude journal (page 62) on colored cardstock paper for each child, scissors, glue, pencils, and crayons.

ACTIVITY: Help children write their personal testimony of Jesus Christ as if they were there when the Savior appeared. Write how they would feel, and how they would show love and gratitude toward the Savior. Then, color journal page.

Review Enrichment Activity #2 (page 119) in Primary 4 manual.*

SCRIPTURE CHALLENGE: Do activity in class or at home.

THOUGHT TREAT: Testimony Time Machine. Break a graham cracker into four parts and glue together with frosting to create an eatable square time machine (or frost crackers together sandwich style). As you eat the cookie, imagine you are going back in time with the Nephites. As you step out of your testimony time machine, imagine that you see Jesus appear to the Nephites. Your testimony increases as you listen to his words. Read: 3 Nephi 11:16-17.

Lesson #34*	**BEATITUDES: Jesus Taught the Nephites** *("Bee"atitude Blessing wheel)*

YOU'LL NEED: Copy of Scripture Challenge card (page 108) and Blessing wheel (pages 63-64) on cardstock paper and a metal or button brad for each child, scissors, glue, and crayons.

ACTIVITY: Create a "Bee"atitude Blessing wheel with Humble Bee, Merciful Bee, Pure in Heart Bee and more, to remind children of the truths Jesus taught the Nephites.

Review Enrichment Activity #1 (page 123) in Primary 4 manual.*

1. Color and cut out "Bee"atitude Blessing wheels.
2. Attach part A on top of part B with a metal brad or button brad (placed in center). TO MAKE BUTTON BRAD: Sew two buttons together on opposite sides (threading thread through the same holes) to attach blessing wheels.

MORE "BEE"ATITUDE FUN: You'll find more beatitude activities in the Ross/King book File Folder Family Home Evenings, (pages 49-55). See the ad in the back of this book to preview the BLESSED BEATITUDES: Jesus Gave the Sermon on the Mount Show-and-Tell presentation and a "Bee"atitude Blockbuster game quiz game.

SCRIPTURE CHALLENGE: Do in class or at home.

THOUGHT TREAT: Honey Taffy. Tell the children that the "bee"atitudes and other truths Jesus taught helped the people to "bee" happy. **TO MAKE TAFFY:** Cook 1 cup honey to boiling stage then medium heat 7-10 minutes, stirring often. Test for crackle stage. Drop 1/2 teaspoon of boiling honey into 1/2 cup cold water. If medium ball forms, it's done. Butter surface and pour honey syrup onto surface to cool 3 minutes. Pull honey into taffy with buttered fingers until light and porous. Cut into pieces and wrap with waxed paper.

If you were there when the Savior appeared, how would you feel? How would you show love and gratitude?

My Personal Testimony of Christ

PATTERN: *BEATITUDES ("Bee"atitude Blessing wheel)*

PATTERN: *BEATITUDES ("Bee"atitude Blessing wheel)*

Lesson #35*	**LOVE: Jesus and Heavenly Father Love Me** *(Guardian angel doorknob reminder)*

YOU'LL NEED: Copy of Scripture Challenge card (page 109) and guardian angel doorknob sign (page 66) on colored cardstock paper for each child, scissors, glue, and crayons.

ACTIVITY: Create a guardian angel to remind each child that Heavenly Father sends ministering angels to them to help them. As they are faithful in keeping their promises, Heavenly Father and Jesus will send comfort and blessings. (1) Color and cut out doorknob sign.

Review Enrichment Activity #1 (page 127) in Primary 4 manual*.

(2) Show children how it fits on the doorknob to remind them that they are loved by Heavenly Father and Jesus, and that guardian angels watch over them.

SCRIPTURE CHALLENGE: Do activity in class or at home.

THOUGHT TREAT: Angel Food Cake. This soft sponge cake can remind children of the soft touch angels have on our lives--since they are around us and we are often not aware of their presence.

Lesson #36*	**SACRAMENT: I Will Remember Jesus** *(sacrament symbols two-sided puzzle)*

YOU'LL NEED: Copy of Scripture Challenge card (page 109) and two-sided puzzle (page 67) on cardstock paper, and an envelope or plastic zip-close bag for each child, scissors, glue, and crayons.

ACTIVITY: Create a sacrament reminder two-sided puzzle to help children always remember Jesus Christ and to strive to have his spirit to be with them.

Review Enrichment Activity #1 (page 130) and Scripture Discussion (pages 129-130) in Primary 4 manual*.

About the Two-Sided Puzzle: Side one of puzzle reminds child of the body (3 Nephi 18:7) and side two reminds child of the blood shed for them (3 Nephi 18:11). Help the children do side 1 puzzle matching the scripture, then side two. Tell them about Jesus bringing the sacrament to the Nephites.

To Make Puzzle: (1) Color and cut out edge of puzzle. (2) Fold puzzle in half on dividing line back-to-back. (3) Glue puzzle together (spreading glue over the entire piece, not just the edges). (4) Trim edges. Cut puzzle shapes out as shown on one side. (5) Place puzzle in an envelope or plastic bag for each child to take home.

SCRIPTURE CHALLENGE: Do activity in class or at home.

THOUGHT TREAT: Unleavened Bread. Bring pita or flat bread and explain that unleavened bread was the bread Jesus gave his disciples in New Testament times and to the Nephites. Unleavened bread is flat bread, unlike the raised yeast bread we have today.

PATTERN: *LOVE*
(guardian angel doorknob reminder)

SACRAMENT SYMBOLS

~~ 3 Nephi 18:7 ~~

And this shall ye do in remembrance of my body, which I have shown unto you. And it shall be a testimony unto the Father that ye do always remember me. And if ye do always remember me ye shall have my Spirit to be with you.

I will remember Jesus.

SACRAMENT SYMBOLS

~~ 3 Nephi 18:11 ~~

And this shall ye always do to those who repent and are baptized in my name; and ye shall do it in remembrance of my blood, which I have shed for you, that ye may witness unto the Father that ye do always remember me. And if ye do always remember me ye shall have my Spirit to be with you.

I will remember Jesus.

| Lesson #37* | **PRAYER Will Protect Me from Temptation**
(Then and Now Challenges obstacle course game) |

YOU'LL NEED: Copy of Scripture Challenge card (page 110) and board game, cards, and Team #1 and #2 markers (pages 69-72) on colored cardstock paper for each child, scissors, glue, crayons, and die (two dice).

ACTIVITY: Play the game that teaches children about prayer THEN (in Nephite Zion) and NOW (today's Zion). The game will take you to these two time periods.

Review Enrichment Activity #1 (page 133) in Primary 4 manual*.

TO MAKE GAME: Color and cut out game board parts A and B, cards, and markers. Glue parts A and B together. **TO PLAY** (see page 72).

SCRIPTURE CHALLENGE: Do activity in class or at home.

THOUGHT TREAT: THEN and NOW Popsicles. Purchase two different flavors of popsicles, break in half and give each child two colors for then and now. Enjoy the two flavors as you think of Book of Mormon times and today.

| Lesson #38* | **HAPPINESS: I Feel Happy as I Live the Teachings of Jesus**
(Happy Choices match game) |

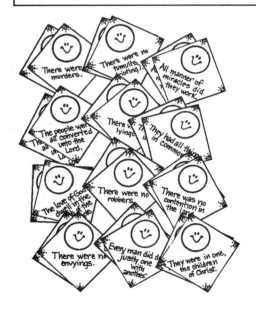

YOU'LL NEED: Copy of Scripture Challenge card (page 110) and two sets of match game cards (page 73) on colored cardstock paper for each child, scissors, pencils, glue, and crayons.

ACTIVITY: Create a Happy Choices match game to show children how the Nephites and Lamanites found peace. Remind children that we too can find peace and happiness as we live the gospel of Jesus Christ. See 4 Nephi 1:2-3, 5, 15-17. Color and cut out cards.

Review Enrichment Activity #1 (page 136) in Primary 4 manual*.

TO PLAY: (1) Divide children into two teams, or children may do activity individually (in this case, each child needs their own set of cards). (2) Lay cards face down and take turns turning two cards over to make a match. (3) When all cards are matched, give one point per card to determine the winning team.

SCRIPTURE CHALLENGE: Do activity in class or at home.

THOUGHT TREAT: Peace Pancakes. Cook two small pancakes side by side connecting in the middle. Squirt jam/jelly from the tube to make a smile on each or write PEACE in the center. Tell children that the Nephites and Lamanites were happy when they found the peace that comes from living the teachings of Jesus.

Then & Now Challenges

HEA... SLIDE! ⬇

SB	If Heavenly Father says "no" to you, know that it is best for YOU!	When you need some special help don't forget to pray!	BB	SLIDE! ⬇
You were sick and felt real bad but thanked Heavenly Father for blessings you had.	Then...		SB	◄ BB
BB				You had no challenges but no blessings either!
SB	Always have a prayer in your heart.	BB	SB	You forgot to pray. Go back 5 spaces.

You followed the example of Jesus and prayed for others!

You forgot to have family prayer. Go back 2 spaces.

 B B

SB

Don't forget to pray.

You ate food without saying a blessing. Go back 2 spaces.

B B

Danger was near and you prayed for help.

 B B

SB

SB

Don't forget to thank Heavenly Father for your many blessings.

 B B

You said the same prayer over & over. Go back to start.

When you pray, say Thee, Thy, Thine & Thou!

 B B

Now!

START!

PATTERN: *PRAYER (Then and Now Challenges Stumbling Block cards)*

STUMBLING BLOCK (THEN & NOW): It's time to get up in the morning and you think of that saying, "Early to bed, early to rise, makes one healthy, wealthy, and wise," but you're tired. WHAT WOULD YOU PRAY ABOUT?	**STUMBLING BLOCK** (THEN): You wanted to go with your friends and build a tree house, but your brother has asked you to help him build a boat to sail to the Promised Land. WHAT WOULD YOU PRAY ABOUT?	**STUMBLING BLOCK** (THEN): You are told by the Lord to build a boat without any windows. You wonder how you can sail without light. WHAT WOULD YOU PRAY ABOUT?
STUMBLING BLOCK (THEN): It's been known for a while that a bright star will shine when Jesus Christ is born. Do you believe what they are saying is true? WHAT WOULD YOU PRAY ABOUT?	**STUMBLING BLOCK** (THEN & NOW): The prophet was telling you to believe in Jesus Christ, and your friends told you to trust in your own thoughts. WHAT WOULD YOU PRAY ABOUT?	**STUMBLING BLOCK** (THEN & NOW): There are others around you who are not living the commandments. They want you to be a part of their plans. You can see that they are becoming more and more wicked. WHAT WOULD YOU PRAY ABOUT?
STUMBLING BLOCK (THEN & NOW): You were asked by the Lord and the prophet to keep a record or journal of your people, and you did not know what to write about. WHAT WOULD YOU PRAY ABOUT?	**STUMBLING BLOCK** (THEN): You are searching for the way to heaven, and others tell you it is found by climbing there. They ask you to help them build a tower. WHAT WOULD YOU PRAY ABOUT?	**STUMBLING BLOCK** (THEN): You are around people who want to fight and kill others. They want you to join their army to take over their enemy's land. WHAT WOULD YOU PRAY ABOUT?
STUMBLING BLOCK (THEN & NOW): Your parents asked you to take care of the house while they are gone. They want you to water the garden and plants and take care of the animals. You are there alone now. WHAT WOULD YOU PRAY ABOUT?	**STUMBLING BLOCK** (THEN & NOW): You are asked to leave your home and leave all the things that you own. You are asked to take your sleeping bag and survival needs. You are asked to do this because your father asked you to. WHAT WOULD YOU PRAY ABOUT?	**STUMBLING BLOCK** (THEN): You were asked to get something from a wicked man, a genealogy, a sacred record that was important to your family. You hesitate, because you don't know if you will come back alive. WHAT WOULD YOU PRAY ABOUT?
STUMBLING BLOCK (THEN & NOW): Your brothers do not listen to the prophet and the words which are in the scriptures. They would rather go their own way and do what they want to do. You want to listen to the prophet and live the commandments. WHAT WOULD YOU PRAY ABOUT?	**STUMBLING BLOCK** (THEN & NOW): Your parents take you to live in a place you have never been. You don't know anyone, and you are not sure you want to live there. You have left all your friends, and you would like to run back to where you came from. WHAT WOULD YOU PRAY ABOUT?	**STUMBLING BLOCK** (THEN & NOW): You have gained knowledge of the scriptures and you know the teachings of Jesus Christ are true. Your friend does not know what you know, and starts asking you questions about what you believe. WHAT WOULD YOU PRAY ABOUT?
STUMBLING BLOCK (THEN & NOW): You haven't been living the teachings of Jesus, and you want your friends to disobey the commandments with you. You have a strong feeling that if you don't repent now, you will never find the truth. WHAT WOULD YOU PRAY ABOUT?	**STUMBLING BLOCK** (THEN & NOW): You know it's time for you to go on a mission and start telling others about the gospel of Jesus Christ. You want to tell others about the gospel, but you are not sure if the words you speak are right. You are afraid that people will laugh at the way you say things. WHAT WOULD YOU PRAY ABOUT?	**STUMBLING BLOCK** (THEN & NOW): Someone needs your help. You ask them what you can do to help, and do it without pay. You are beginning to build a friendship. This person is beginning to trust you and want you for a friend. You feel it's time to talk about the gospel, but you wait. WHAT WOULD YOU PRAY ABOUT?

PATTERN: *PRAYER (Then and Now Challenges game Blessing Bonus cards)*

BLESSING BONUS:	BLESSING BONUS:	BLESSING BONUS:
You went the extra mile today. You stopped, you looked, you listened, and you did obey. MOVE FORWARD ONE STEP.	You've done a lot of work, you did not shirk, you put your shoulder to the wheel. Ask the members of your team to yell "HIP HIP HOORAY!"	Blessings are in store forever more because you are a faithful Saint. Take each blessing one by one and count what God has done. BEGIN COUNTING NOW!
BLESSING BONUS: Your mother is a dear, she gives you lots of cheer. You deserve the best, so give your mother some rest and SAY MOTHER DEAR, I LOVE YOU!	**BLESSING BONUS:** Blessings unnumbered await you today, as you have chosen the righteous way. CONSIDER YOURSELF BLESSED!	**BLESSING BONUS:** Look at what you've got, not what you have not. Look at those who are less fortunate than you and decide just what you can do to help. MAKE A LIST.
BLESSING BONUS: It's about time you found the time to tell yourself that you are terrific! Say it now! "I'M TERRIF!" MOVE AHEAD ONE.	**BLESSING BONUS:** Not one, not two, but eternal blessings true. They wait for you as you pursue...living the gospel of Jesus Christ. MOVE AHEAD ONE.	**BLESSING BONUS:** If you want to move forward in this game, just name it, you can choose. Roll the dice and move any number between 1 and 4. ROLL DICE AND MOVE.
BLESSING BONUS: Ever since you were in the crib, you wanted to say, "goo goo," so say it now while you have an audience true! "GOO GOO DA DA MA MA!" MOVE AHEAD ONE SPACE.	**BLESSING BONUS:** Farewell to troubles, farewell to gloom, you have entered the happiness room. Each time you pray you can say you chose the righteous way. Say "Amen," and MOVE AHEAD ONE. AMEN.	**BLESSING BONUS:** As you are living the teachings of the living prophet—having family home evening, reading scriptures, having family and personal prayers, paying tithing, and attending church—MOVE AHEAD TWO.
BLESSING BONUS: It's no joke you are not a slowpoke. You sped on past the other guys in your class! MOVE AHEAD TWO SPACES.	**BLESSING BONUS:** Give me a nickel, give me a dime, money means nothing when it's going to heaven time! You can't take earthly treasures with you, so dig deep for heavenly treasures that are safe to keep. MOVE AHEAD FOUR SPACES.	**BLESSING BONUS:** For praying with an honest heart and doing your best to do your part, MOVE AHEAD TWO SPACES.
BLESSING BONUS: Blessing Bonanza! The Book of Mormon tells of people who were blessed when they were righteous. They prayed, lived the commandments and really made the grade! For living like the righteous Nephites and Lamanites, MOVE ONE.	**BLESSING BONUS:** Think of THEN in Book of Mormon times and think of NOW and how you're blessed, and how! Name one of your blessings and MOVE AHEAD ONE.	**BLESSING BONUS:** You want to win, your team is pushing ahead. Take a deep breath and MOVE AHEAD TWO SPACES!.

THEN & NOW CHALLENGES GAME

HOW TO PLAY: ♥ Put Stumbling Block cards and Blessing Bonus cards face down in separate piles. ♥ Divide players into two teams or play individually. Place marker on board at START. Take turns rolling die and moving marker on board toward HEAVEN. ♥ Draw a Stumbling Block card when you land on SB. Answer what you would pray about to make a decision living THEN in Nephite Zion or NOW in Today's Zion. ♥ Draw a Blessing Bonus card when you land on BB (move or do as it says). ♥ First one to reach HEAVEN wins! Or, play until all cards are read.

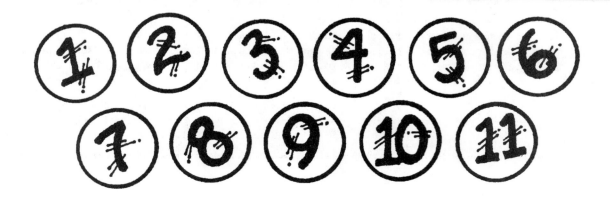

HAPPY CHOICES MATCH GAME: Learn of the happy choices the Nephites and Lamanites made to have peace. Take turns turning cards over to make a match. When all cards are matched, count the matches to determine the winner.
4 Nephi 1:2-3, 5, 15-17

Every man did deal justly one with another.

The love of God did dwell in the ♡'s of the people.

There were no envyings.

They had all things in common.

All manner of miracles did they work.

There was no contention in the land.

There were no robbers.

They were all one, the children of Christ.

The people were all converted unto the Lord.

There were no murders.

There were no tumults (rioting).

There were no lyings.

Lesson #39*

HONOR: I Will Be True to the Teachings of Jesus
(Book of Mormon Honor Roll merit match)

YOU'LL NEED: Copy of Scripture Challenge card (page 111) and merit match and glue-on stickers (pages 75-76) on colored cardstock paper for each guest, scissors, glue, and crayons.

ACTIVITY: Remind children to be true to the teachings of Jesus as they create an Honor Roll to spotlight Book of Mormon heroes. In spite of the evils that were around them, these men were true to the teachings of Jesus. Mormon kept the records, thus bringing these Honor Roll examples to us (Mormon 1:4-5).

Review Enrichment Activity #4 (page 140) in Primary 4 manual*.

1. Color and cut out Honor Roll glue-on stickers.
2. Read the scriptures and descriptions in the boxes and match a hero picture.
3. Glue only top of picture over "HERO" tab to flip up.

TO FIND HEROES: Read descriptions in the Book of Mormon Index. Place pictures as shown above.

SCRIPTURE CHALLENGE: Do activity in class or at home.

THOUGHT TREAT: Honor Cake Roll. Make or purchase ice cream cake roll. Say to the children, "This cake roll is like the pages of the Book of Mormon. If the pages were attached and rolled out together, you would find that: 1) Each hero shares his testimony of Jesus Christ. 2) Each hero is valiant in living the teachings of Jesus.

Lesson #40*

HOLY GHOST Will Guide Me
(Jaredite crossword puzzle)

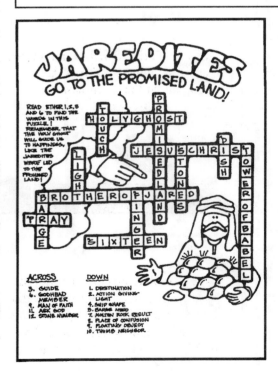

YOU'LL NEED: Copy of Scripture Challenge card (page 111) and crossword puzzle and Thought Treat placemat (pages 77-78) on cardstock paper for each child, scissors, pencil, glue, and crayons.

ACTIVITY: Read Ether 1, 2, 3, and 6 to find the words in the puzzle. Remember that the Holy Ghost will guide us to happiness, like the Jaredites who were lead to the promised land.

Review Scripture Account and Discussion (pages 141-142) in Primary 4 manual*.

ANSWERS--ACROSS: (3) Holy Ghost (6) Jesus Christ (9) brother of Jared (11) pray (12) sixteen DOWN: (1) promised land (2) touch (4) dish (5) light (7) stones (8) tower of Babel (9) barge (10) finger

SCRIPTURE CHALLENGE: Do activity in class or at home.

THOUGHT TREAT: Cookie Barge (Boat). Copy, color and cut out body of water placemat to place a Jaredite-like Cookie Barge (Boat) inside. Talk about the barge they sailed in to the Promised Land (shaped like a dish) having no windows. Jared prayed for guidance on how to sail without light or air. Read Ether 2:17 for description). ***TO MAKE COOKIE BARGE:*** ♥ Preheat oven to 375° and grease cookie sheet. ♥ Beat an 18-ounce cake mix, 3/4 cup water, and 2 eggs. Drop batter with heaping tablespoon on cookie sheet 3 inches apart. ♥ Bake 8-11 minutes or until puffed and golden brown. Cool and frost cookie bottoms (not top), placing bottoms together like a sandwich (or shaped like a double dish upside down).

I Will Be True to the Teachings of Jesus
HONOR ROLL

Let's honor heroes of the Book of Mormon. Read the scriptures in boxes and match a hero picture.
Glue only top of picture over "HERO" tab to flip up.   These men were true to the teachings of Jesus.

HERO (glue picture top here):

I tried to destroy the church with the sons of Mosiah. An angel told me to repent. I did repent and then became a mighty missionary.
Alma 36:6-9

HERO (glue picture top here):

I am a son of Mosiah. I was a missionary to King Lamoni and to the Lamanites. Those who were brought to the knowledge of the truth, through my preaching, never fell away.
Alma 23:6

HERO (glue picture top here):

I am the son of Alma. I was a prophet and military commander. I guided the 2,000 stripling warriors fighting for peace. I was entrusted with plates to keep a record. I was given the 24 plates of Jaredites.
Alma 56:47-48, 56

HERO (glue picture top here):

Because of my faith, I was led to the Land of Promise which is choice above all other lands. My father was a prophet.
1 Nephi 2:19-20

HERO (glue picture top here):

I was the son of Mormon. I recorded my father's teachings of faith, hope, and charity. I was the last living Nephite. I finished the record of my father and sealed up the plates. I wrote the Book of Mormon Promise.
Moroni 10:4-5

HERO (glue picture top here):

I am a Nephite prophet. I taught that Jesus is the light and life of the world, a light that is endless.
Mosiah 16:9

HERO (glue picture top here):

I am a Nephite prophet. I organized the Church of Jesus and baptized many saints in the Waters of Mormon. I commanded the people to share their substance.
Mosiah 18:5-8

HERO (glue picture top here):

I was chief captain of the Nephite armies. I inspired the soldiers to fight for freedom. I made a title of liberty for those who were true believers in Jesus. I and my people supported the cause of freedom.
Alma 46:12-15

HERO (glue picture top here):

I was a Nephite prophet. I abridged the large plates of Nephi and put the small plates with them. I prayed that the plates would be preserved. The Nephites would not let me preach to them.
Words of Mormon 1:11

PATTERN: HONOR (Book of Mormon Honor Roll merit match "HERO" pictures)

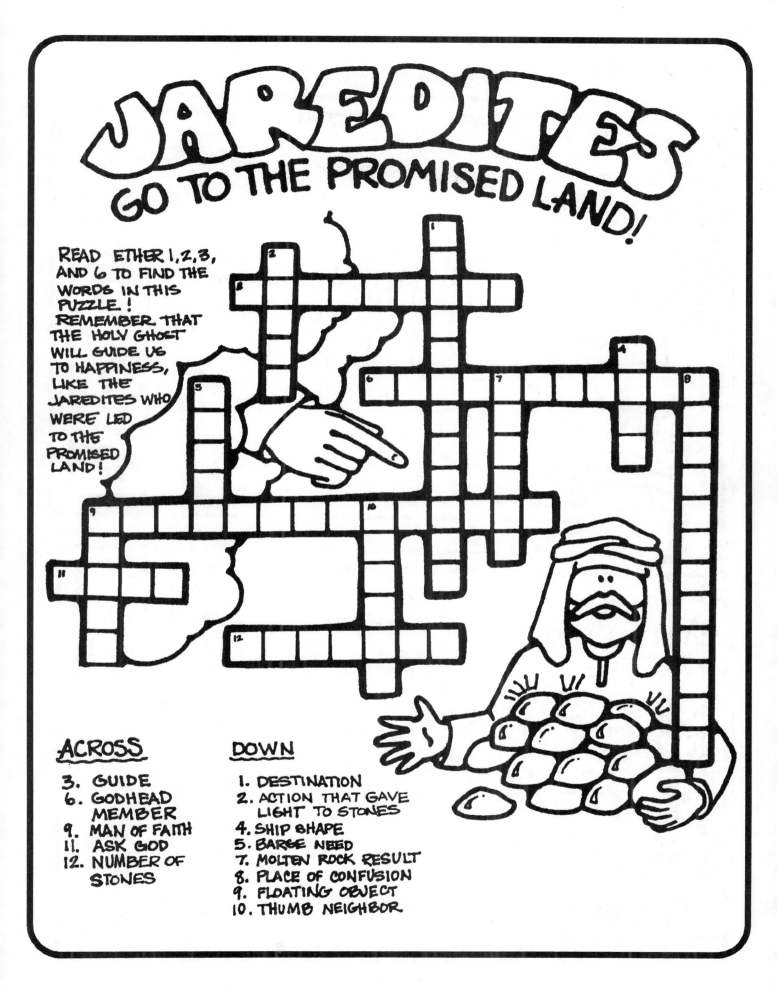

JAREDITES
GO TO THE PROMISED LAND!

READ ETHER 1,2,3, AND 6 TO FIND THE WORDS IN THIS PUZZLE! REMEMBER THAT THE HOLY GHOST WILL GUIDE US TO HAPPINESS, LIKE THE JAREDITES WHO WERE LED TO THE PROMISED LAND!

ACROSS

3. GUIDE
6. GODHEAD MEMBER
9. MAN OF FAITH
11. ASK GOD
12. NUMBER OF STONES

DOWN

1. DESTINATION
2. ACTION THAT GAVE LIGHT TO STONES
4. SHIP SHAPE
5. BARGE NEED
7. MOLTEN ROCK RESULT
8. PLACE OF CONFUSION
9. FLOATING OBJECT
10. THUMB NEIGHBOR

PATTERN: *HOLY GHOST (Cookie Barge Thought Treat placemat)*

Lesson #41*	**PROPHETS: I Will Listen to the Prophet to Stay in the Light**
	(Cycle of history wheel)

YOU'LL NEED: Copy of Scripture Challenge card (page 112) and cycle of history wheel parts A and B (pages 80-81) on colored cardstock paper, and a metal or button brad for each child, scissors, and crayons.

ACTIVITY: Create a cycle of history wheel that children can share with their families to encourage them to listen to the prophet and stay in the light. Wheel arrow turns from dark to light side to show where they can find the light. (1) Color and cut out parts A and B. (2) Attach part A on top of part B with a metal or button brad (placed in the center). (3) To Make Button Brad: Sew two buttons together on opposite sides (threading thread through the same hole) to attach wheel parts A and B. (4) To use wheel see page 68 for details.

Review Enrichment Activity #3 (page 146) in Primary 4 manual*.

SCRIPTURE CHALLENGE: Do activity in class or at home.

THOUGHT TREAT: Sunshine Cookie. Decorate round sugar cookies with sunny yellow frosting, and decorate by drawing an arrow with contrasting frosting. Tell children as they follow the straight and narrow path, staying in the light, they will find blessings.

Lesson #42*	**CHARITY: I Choose the Pure Love of Christ**
	(Moroni and Me personal golden plates)

YOU'LL NEED: Copy of Scripture Challenge card (page 112) and Moroni and Me personal golden plates (pages 82-83) on cardstock paper for each child, pencils, and crayons.

ACTIVITY: Create your own set of golden plates and follow the example of Moroni. Help the children learn about Moroni and how he showed charity, the pure love of Jesus Christ. Challenge children to complete Days 1-12 charity challenges.

Review Enrichment Activity #3 (page 150) in Primary 4 manual*.

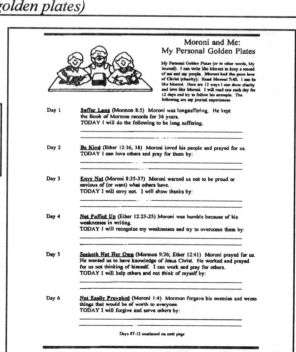

SCRIPTURE CHALLENGE: Do activity in class or at home.

THOUGHT TREAT: Charity Cookies. Make a plate of cookies children can help you deliver to someone special (a widow or widower, or a special family needing love and attention). P.S. Children can deliver these as a group and enjoy eating a cookie (made just for them) on the way. Memorize "Moroni 7:47" along the way.

PATTERN: *PROPHETS*
(cycle of history wheel Part A)

TO USE WHEEL: Read the
scriptures below. Turn the arrow to the
place in time found in the scripture.
Notice if the people were in the light or
the dark cycle in history.
♥ The prophets warn us to think about
our own lives and where we are in the
cycle of history. Ask yourself: What
can I do to turn
toward the light?

SCRIPTURES:
4 Nephi 1:18
Alma 7:17
Ether 10:28
Alma 4:12
1 Nephi 7:20
3 Nephi 10:18
Helaman 3:25-26
Ether 6:12
Helaman 6:1
Enos 1:4-5
Alma 4:1-3
3 Nephi 2:3
4 Nephi 1:24
Helaman 4:15
Alma 8:14
3 Nephi 8:25
Alma 48:20
Helaman 12:1

SCRIPTURES:
4 Nephi 1:18
Alma 7:17
Ether 10:28
Alma 4:12
1 Nephi 7:20
3 Nephi 10:18
Helaman 3:25-26
Ether 6:12
Helaman 6:1
Enos 1:4-5
Alma 4:1-3
3 Nephi 2:3
4 Nephi 1:24
Helaman 4:15
Alma 8:14
3 Nephi 8:25
Alma 48:20
Helaman 12:1

TO USE WHEEL: Read the
scriptures below. Turn the arrow to the
place in time found in the scripture.
Notice if the people were in the light or
the dark cycle in history.
♥ The prophets warn us to think about
our own lives and where we are in the
cycle of history. Ask yourself: What
can I do to turn
toward the light?

PATTERN: *PROPHETS (cycle of history wheel Part B)*

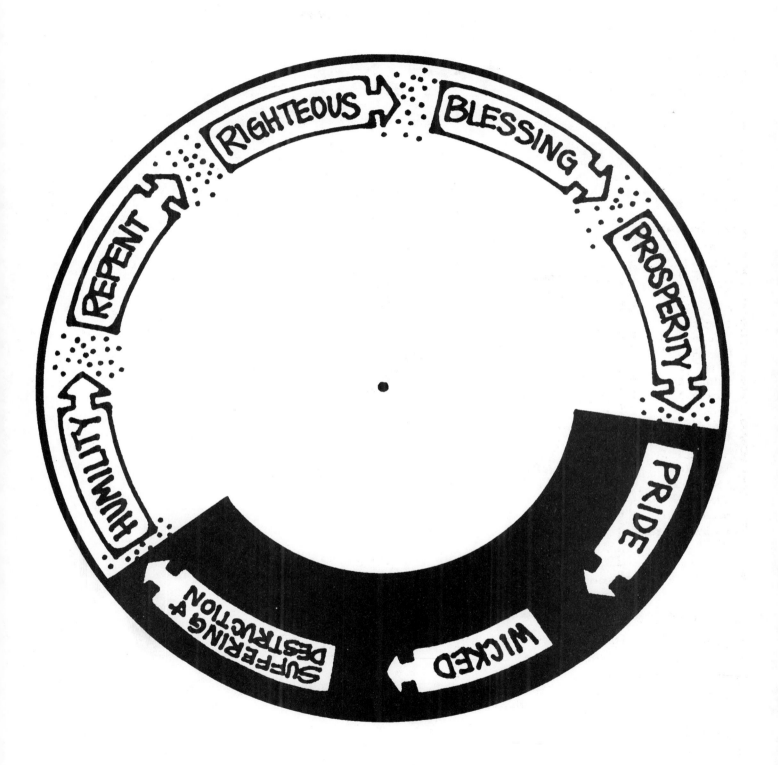

Moroni and Me:
My Personal Golden Plates

My Personal Golden Plates (or in other words, My Journal): I can write like Moroni to keep a record of me and my people. **Moroni had the pure love of Christ (charity): Read Moroni 7:45.** I can be like Moroni. Here are 12 ways I can show charity and love like Moroni. I will read one each day for 12 days and try to follow his example. The following are my journal experiences.

Day 1   <u>**Suffer Long**</u> (Mormon 8:5) Moroni was long-suffering. He kept the Book of Mormon records for 36 years.
TODAY I will do the following to be long-suffering:

_____

_____

Day 2   <u>**Be Kind**</u> (Ether 12:36, 38) Moroni loved his people and prayed for us.
TODAY I can love others and pray for them by:

_____

_____

Day 3   <u>**Envy Not**</u> (Moroni 8:35-37) Moroni warned us not to be proud or envious of (or want) what others have.
TODAY I will envy not. I will show thanks by:

_____

_____

Day 4   <u>**Not Puffed Up**</u> (Ether 12:23-25) Moroni was humble because of his weaknesses in writing.
TODAY I will recognize my weaknesses and try to overcome them by:

_____

_____

Day 5   <u>**Seeketh Not Her Own**</u> (Mormon 9:36; Ether 12:41) Moroni prayed for us. He wanted us to have a knowledge of Jesus Christ. He worked and prayed for us, not thinking of himself. I can work and pray for others.
TODAY I will help others and not think of myself by:

_____

_____

Day 6   <u>**Not Easily Provoked**</u> (Moroni 1:4) Mormon forgave his enemies and wrote things that would be of worth to everyone.
TODAY I will forgive and serve others by:

_____

_____

Days #7-12 continued on next page

Moroni and Me:
My Personal Golden Plates

CONTINUED Days #7-12 Charity Challenges
Inspired by Moroni
*"Except men shall have charity they cannot inherit
that place thou hast prepared in the mansion of
thy Father."* (Ether 12:34)

Day 7   **<u>Thinketh No Evil</u>**
(Moroni 10:30) Moroni said to "come
unto Christ, and lay hold upon every good gift and touch
not the evil gift, nor the unclean thing.
TODAY I will seek after good things and avoid evil or unclean things by:

_____

_____

Day 8   **<u>Rejoice in Truth</u>** (Moroni 10:27) Moroni rejoiced in truth. He was
honest in his dealings with others and in his writings.
TODAY I will show honesty by:

_____

_____

Day 9   **<u>Beareth All Things</u>** (Moroni 1:2-3) Moroni wandered alone for many
years. Even to save his life he would not deny Jesus Christ.
TODAY I will bear my testimony to others in what I do by:

_____

_____

Day 10   **<u>Believeth All Things</u>** (Mormon 9:21) Moroni said that if we believe in Jesus Christ,
doubting nothing, we will receive what we ask for.
TODAY I will believe in Jesus Christ and pray for:

_____

Moroni's faith allowed him to see Jesus face to face. (Ether 12:39).

Day 11   **<u>Hopeth All Things</u>** (Ether 12:32) Moroni said that if we don't have hope,
we cannot receive an inheritance in the mansions of heaven.
TODAY I will hope and try to reach for:

_____

_____

Day 12   **<u>Endureth All Things</u>** (Moroni 10:34) Moroni was faithful to the teachings of Jesus Christ
to the end of his life. He will rest in paradise and asks us to meet him there to live with God
our Eternal Judge.
TODAY I will endure to the end and do the best I can at:

_____

_____

Lesson #43*	**FAITH:** I Will Be Strong in Faith
	(Faith-ful Saints guessing game)

YOU'LL NEED: Copy of Scripture Challenge card (page 113) and guessing game pictures and clue cards (pages 85-86) on colored cardstock paper, scissors, glue, and crayons.

ACTIVITY: To encourage children to exercise their faith in Jesus Christ, play the Faith-ful Saints guessing game.

Review Enrichment Activities #1-2 (pages 153-154) in Primary 4 manual.*

TO MAKE GAME: (1) Color and cut out pictures and clue cards. (2) Lay picture cards on the floor or table face up. (3) Lay clue cards in a pile face down. **TO PLAY:** Divide into two teams and take turns drawing a clue card. Read the Faith-ful Saint description and guess which picture card it matches. If the guess is wrong, the other team has a chance to guess. When the guess is right, that team collects the matching picture and cue card. The team with the most cards wins.

ANSWERS TO CLUES #1-12: (1) Enos   (2) Alma   (3) Captain Moroni   (4) Ishmael   (5) Nephi (6) Brother of Jared   (7) 2,000 stripling warriors   (8) Ammon   (9) Alma and Amulek   (10) Abinadi (11) Three Nephites   (12) Lehi

SCRIPTURE CHALLENGE: Do activity in class or at home.

THOUGHT TREAT: Testimony Popcorn Balls. To make popcorn balls, cook 2 tablespoons butter, 1½ cups brown sugar, and 5-6 tablespoons water (boiling 3-6 minutes to softball stage). Pour over 4-6 cups popped popcorn and form balls. Tell children that corn is the seed for popcorn. Warm the corn and the popcorn pops. Warm your faith and a testimony "pops" into your life.

Lesson #44*	**TESTIMONY:** Book of Mormon Promise
	(bite-size memorize Moroni 10:4-5)

YOU'LL NEED: Copy of Scripture Challenge card (page 113) and bite-size memorize poster (page 87) on colored cardstock paper for each child, scissors, glue, and crayons.

Review Discussion (page 157) and Testimony (page 159) in Primary 4 manual.*

ACTIVITY: Encourage children to memorize the Book of Mormon promise (Moroni 10:4-5) to gain a personal testimony of the Book of Mormon, to study and live its teachings.

SCRIPTURE CHALLENGE: Do activity in class or at home.

THOUGHT TREAT: Cross Your Heart Pretzels. Enjoy crossed pretzels to remind children that to cross their heart means to faithfully promise. Encourage children to read the scriptures and try the Book of Mormon promise).

*Primary 4 manual is published by The Church of Jesus Christ of Latter-day Saints, Salt Lake City, Utah.

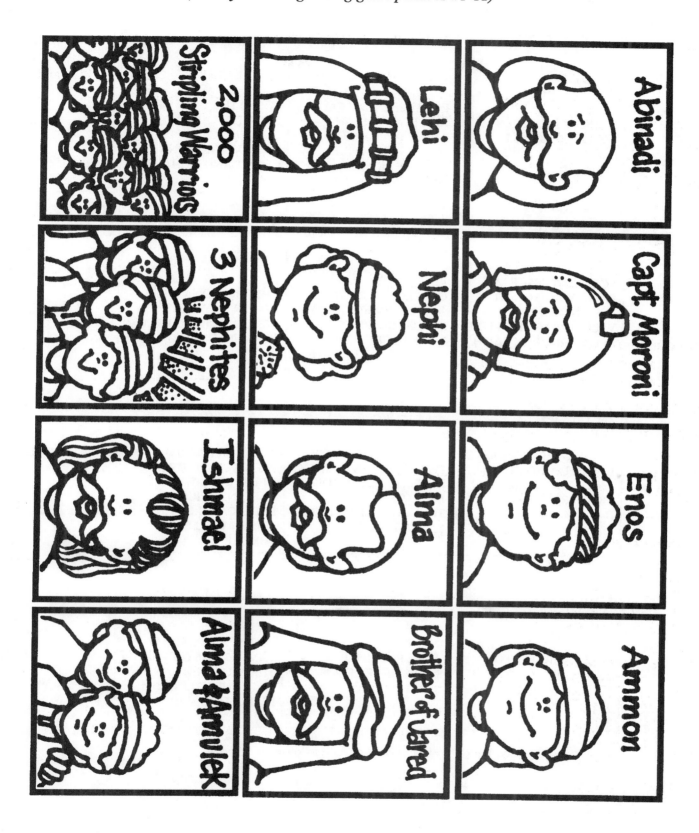

PATTERN: *FAITH (Faithful Saints Guessing Game clues #1-12)*

CLUE #1: I USED MY FAITH IN JESUS CHRIST AS I PRAYED DAY AND NIGHT.	**CLUE #2:** BECAUSE OF MY FAITH AND PRAYERS, AN ANGEL APPEARED TO MY SON AND FOUR SONS OF MOSIAH, CALLING THEM TO REPENTANCE.	**CLUE #3:** I USED THE TITLE OF LIBERTY FLAG TO ENCOURAGE MY PEOPLE TO HAVE FAITH IN JESUS CHRIST AND FIGHT FOR LIBERTY.
CLUE #4: I CHOSE TO TAKE MY FAMILY AND GO WITH LEHI INTO THE WILDERNESS. THIS I DID BECAUSE OF MY FAITH.	**CLUE #5:** I HAD FAITH THAT I COULD RETURN TO JERUSALEM TO GET THE BRASS PLATES. THESE WERE SACRED RECORDS KEPT BY THE PROPHETS.	**CLUE #6:** I HAD FAITH IN JESUS CHRIST AND SAW HIS FINGER. MY FAITH INCREASED AND I SAW HIS WHOLE BEING.
CLUE #7 OUR MOTHERS TAUGHT US TO HAVE FAITH. OUR FAITH TAUGHT BY OUR MOTHERS SAVED US IN BATTLE.	**CLUE #8** I DESIRED TO PREACH THE GOSPEL. MY FAITH HELPED ME FIGHT OFF A BAND OF ROBBERS TRYING TO KILL KING LAMONI'S SHEEP.	**CLUE #9:** WHILE TRYING TO PREACH REPENTANCE IN THE CITY, WE WERE CAST INTO PRISON. OUR FAITH CAUSED THE PRISON WALLS TO TUMBLE.
CLUE #10: BECAUSE OF MY FAITH IN JESUS CHRIST, I WAS WILLING TO DIE FOR MY TESTIMONY (AT THE HANDS OF KING NOAH).	**CLUE #11:** BECAUSE OF OUR FAITH IN JESUS CHRIST, WE WERE PROMISED WE SHALL NEVER FACE DEATH.	**CLUE #12:** BECAUSE OF OUR FAITH IN JESUS CHRIST, MY FAMILY WAS GUIDED TO THE PROMISED LAND, WITH THE HELP OF THE LIAHONA.

ANSWERS found on page 84 or in the following scriptures:

Clue #1 Enos 1:3-4   Clue #2 Alma 36:6-10   Clue #3 Alma 46:12-13   Clue #4 I Nephi 7:2, 4-5

Clue #5 I Nephi 4:1-31   Clue #6 Ether 3, 12:30   Clue #7 Alma 56:44-56   Clue #8 Alma 17:29-18:3, 26:12

Clue #9 Alma 14:26-28   Clue #10 Mosiah 17:7-20   Clue #11 3 Nephi 28:1-7   Clue #12 1 Nephi 16:28-29; 18:23

BITE SIZE MEMORIZE

Moroni 10:4-5

And when ye shall receive these things, I would exhort you that ye would ask God the Eternal Father in the name of Christ, if these things are not true; and if ye shall ask with a sincere heart, with real intent, having faith in Christ, he will manifest the truth of it unto you, by the power of the Holy Ghost.

And by the power of the Holy Ghost ye may know the truth of all things.

Lesson #45*	**EASTER:** Book of Mormon Testifies of the Resurrection
	(He Has Risen write-a-story)

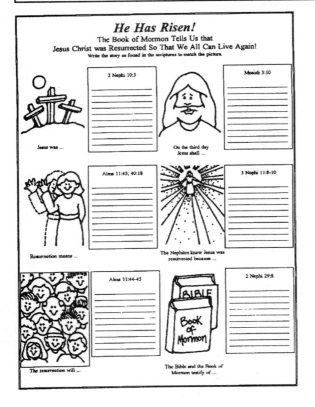

He Has Risen!
The Book of Mormon Tells Us that
Jesus Christ was Resurrected So That We All Can Live Again!
Write the story as found in the scriptures to match the picture.

2 Nephi 10:3

Jesus was ...

Mosiah 3:10

On the third day
Jesus shall ...

Alma 11:43; 40:18

Resurrection means ...

3 Nephi 11:8-10

The Nephites knew Jesus was
resurrected because ...

Alma 11:44-45

The resurrection will ...

2 Nephi 29:8

The Bible and the Book of
Mormon testify of ...

YOU'LL NEED: Copy Scripture Challenge card (page 114) and He Has Risen write-a-story activity (page 89) on cardstock paper for each guest, scissors, pencils, glue, and crayons.

ACTIVITY: Encourage children to write their own Easter picture story showing that the Book of Mormon is another testament of Jesus Christ and the resurrection.
1. Color the pictures.
2. Help children look up the scripture and write the story that matches the picture in their own words.

Review Enrichment Activity #1 and Testimony (page 162) in Primary 4 manual.*

SCRIPTURE CHALLENGE: Do activity in class or at home.

THOUGHT TREAT: Easter Egg Hunt. Hide and find candy and boiled colored eggs. Tell the children that the eggs symbolize new life or a new beginning. Jesus brought us all new life or a new beginning. Because he died for us and was resurrected, we will be able to be forgiven of our sins, if we repent, and we will be able to live again. After we die we will be resurrected just as Jesus was; we will have a new body when Jesus comes again. Read Alma 33:22.

Lesson #46*	**CHRISTMAS:** Book of Mormon: Another Witness of Jesus
	(Signs of His Coming star ornament)

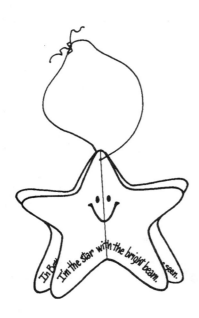

In Bethlehem a star with the bright beam was seen.

YOU'LL NEED: Copy of Scripture Challenge card (page 114) and star ornament (page 90) on colored cardstock paper for each child, scissors, glue, crayons, and 12" piece of string or ribbon.

ACTIVITY: Show the children that the Bible is one witness of Jesus Christ and the Book of Mormon is

Review Scripture Account and Discussion (page 164) in Primary 4 manual.*

another witness, showing signs of his birth. Search the scriptures to find the signs of Jesus Christ's birth seen in Bethlehem and in America (Luke 2:6-14; Matthew 2:1-2, and 3 Nephi 1:21), and other signs given in America.
TO MAKE ORNAMENT: Cut out stars, fold back to back and glue. Poke hole at top, string thread through and tie to hang on tree.

SCRIPTURE CHALLENGE CARD: Do in class or at home.

THOUGHT TREAT: Open Face Cheese Star Sandwich. Cut out a slice of bread and American cheese in star shape. Place cheese on top of bread to serve). Tell children that the star in the sky was a sign that Jesus Christ is born.

*Primary 4 manual is published by The Church of Jesus Christ of Latter-day Saints, Salt Lake City, Utah.

He Has Risen!

The Book of Mormon Tells Us That
Jesus Christ Was Resurrected So That We All Can Live Again!

Write the story as found in the scriptures to match the picture.

Jesus was ...

2 Nephi 10:3

_____
_____
_____
_____
_____
_____
_____
_____

On the third day
Jesus shall ...

Mosiah 3:10

_____
_____
_____
_____
_____
_____
_____
_____

Resurrection means ...

Alma 11:43; 40:18

_____
_____
_____
_____
_____
_____
_____
_____
_____

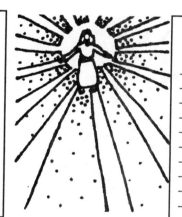

The Nephites knew Jesus was
resurrected because ...

3 Nephi 11:8-10

_____
_____
_____
_____
_____
_____
_____
_____
_____

The resurrection will ...

Alma 11:44-45

_____
_____
_____
_____
_____
_____
_____
_____

The Bible and the Book of
Mormon testify of ...

2 Nephi 29:8

_____
_____
_____
_____
_____
_____
_____

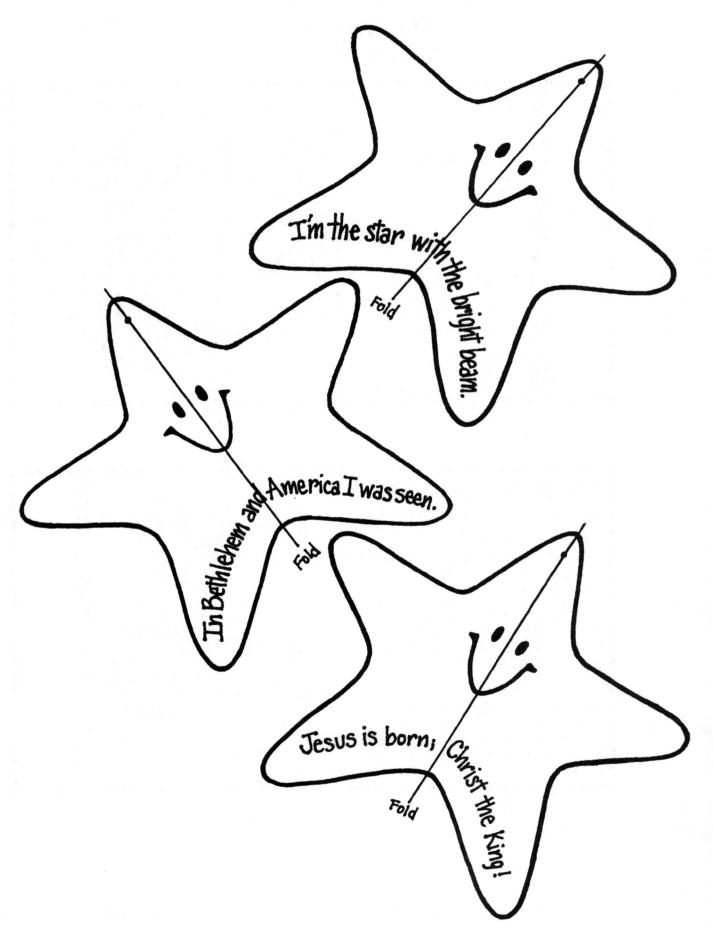

Front and back cover for Scripture Challenge cards #1-46
to match lesson #1-46 in Primary 4* manual.

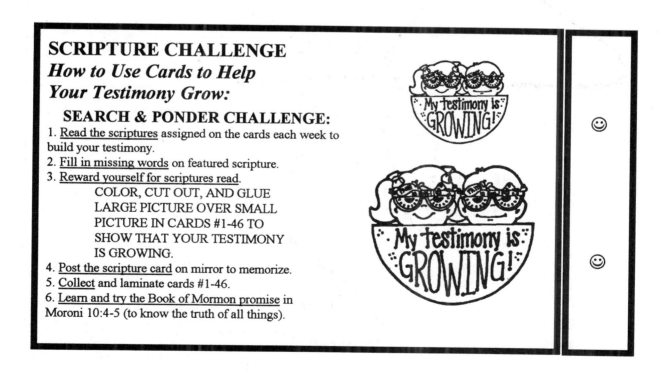

My Scripture Challenge Cards

Year:

_____

Cards Belong To:

_____

_____

FAITH IS COOL!

SCRIPTURE CHALLENGE
How to Use Cards to Help Your Testimony Grow:

SEARCH & PONDER CHALLENGE:

1. <u>Read the scriptures</u> assigned on the cards each week to build your testimony.
2. <u>Fill in missing words</u> on featured scripture.
3. <u>Reward yourself for scriptures read</u>.
    COLOR, CUT OUT, AND GLUE LARGE PICTURE OVER SMALL PICTURE IN CARDS #1-46 TO SHOW THAT YOUR TESTIMONY IS GROWING.
4. <u>Post the scripture card</u> on mirror to memorize.
5. <u>Collect</u> and laminate cards #1-46.
6. <u>Learn and try the Book of Mormon promise</u> in Moroni 10:4-5 (to know the truth of all things).

BOOK OF MORMON:

#1

Another Testament of Jesus Christ

SEARCH & PONDER CHALLENGE:
Read This Week: Joseph Smith--History
1:29-35 42-54, 59-60

Joseph Smith was inspired to pray after
he read **James 1:5**:
"If any of you lack __ __ __ __ __ __,
let him ask of __ __ __, that giveth to all
men __ __ __ __ __ __ __ __ __ __, and
upbraideth not; and it shall be
__ __ __ __ __ him."

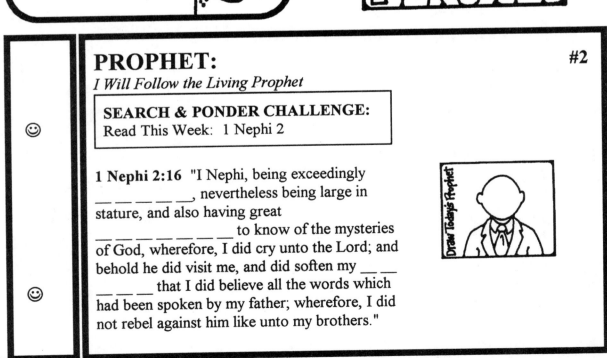

PROPHET:

#2

I Will Follow the Living Prophet

SEARCH & PONDER CHALLENGE:
Read This Week: 1 Nephi 2

1 Nephi 2:16 "I Nephi, being exceedingly
__ __ __ __ __ __, nevertheless being large in
stature, and also having great
__ __ __ __ __ __ __ __ to know of the mysteries
of God, wherefore, I did cry unto the Lord; and
behold he did visit me, and did soften my __ __
__ __ __ that I did believe all the words which
had been spoken by my father; wherefore, I did
not rebel against him like unto my brothers."

COMMANDMENTS:
Heavenly Father Helps Me as I Obey

#3

SEARCH & PONDER CHALLENGE:
Read This Week: 1 Nephi 3:1-8, 4

1 Nephi 3:7 "I, Nephi, said unto my father: I will __ __ and __ __ the things which the Lord hath __ __ __ __ __ __ __ __ __ __, for I know that the Lord __ __ __ __ __ __ no commandments unto the children of men, save he shall __ __ __ __ __ __ __ __ a way for them that they may accomplish the thing which he commanded them."

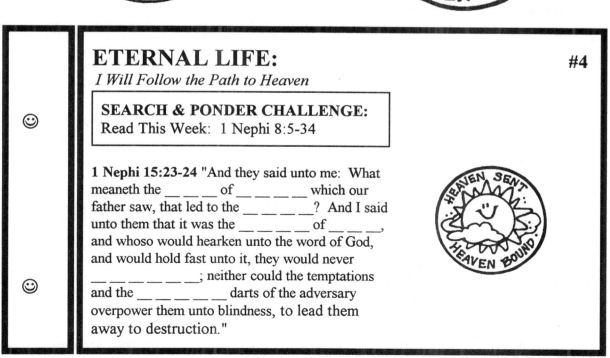

ETERNAL LIFE:
I Will Follow the Path to Heaven

#4

SEARCH & PONDER CHALLENGE:
Read This Week: 1 Nephi 8:5-34

1 Nephi 15:23-24 "And they said unto me: What meaneth the __ __ __ of __ __ __ __ which our father saw, that led to the __ __ __ __? And I said unto them that it was the __ __ __ __ of __ __ __, and whoso would hearken unto the word of God, and would hold fast unto it, they would never __ __ __ __ __ __; neither could the temptations and the __ __ __ __ __ darts of the adversary overpower them unto blindness, to lead them away to destruction."

TRUST: #5
Heavenly Father Will Guide Me

SEARCH & PONDER CHALLENGE:
Read This Week: 1 Nephi 16:18-32

1 Nephi 16:10 "And it came to pass that as my father arose in the morning, and went forth to the tent door, to his great astonishment he beheld upon the ground a round _ _ _ _ of curious workmanship; and it was of fine _ _ _ _ _ _. And within the ball were _ _ _ spindles; and the one _ _ _ _ _ _ _ the way whither we should go into the wilderness."

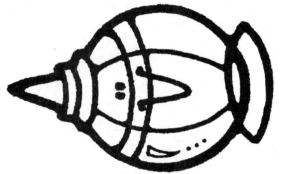

EXAMPLE: #6
I Will Be a Good Example to Others

SEARCH & PONDER CHALLENGE:
Read This Week: 1 Nephi 17:3-22, 45-55

1 Nephi 17:3 "The commandments of God must be fulfilled. And if it so be that the children of men keep the commandments of God he doth _ _ _ _ _ _ _ _ them, and strengthen them, and provide means whereby they can accomplish the thing which he has commanded them; wherefore, he did provide means for us while we did sojourn in the _ _ _ _ _ _ _ _ _ _ _."

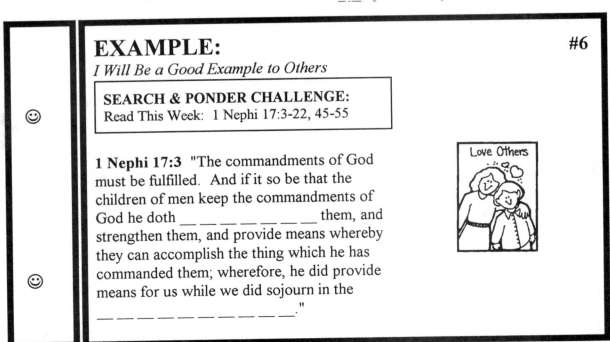

Love Others

HOLY GHOST: #7
I Want to Be Worthy to Receive His Spirit

SEARCH & PONDER CHALLENGE:
Read This Week: 1 Nephi 18:5-25

Like the Liahona, we are given the Holy Ghost to guide us. **1 Nephi 18:12, 21** "After they had bound me insomuch that I could not move, the
__ __ __ __ __ __ __ [Liahona], which had been prepared of the Lord, did cease to work ... After they had loosed me, behold, I took the
__ __ __ __ __ __ __, and it did work whither I desired it ... I prayed ... and ... the storm did cease, and there was a great __ __ __ __."

TESTIMONY: #8
I Will Strengthen My Testimony of Jesus

SEARCH & PONDER CHALLENGE:
Read This Week: Jacob 7:1-23

Jacob 7:12
"And this is not all--it has been made manifest unto me, for I have __ __ __ __ __ and seen; and it has also been made manifest unto me by the __ __ __ __ __ of the Holy Ghost; wherefore, I know if there should be no atonement made all mankind must be __ __ __ __."

PRAYER:
I Can Pray for Blessings

#9

SEARCH & PONDER CHALLENGE:
Read This Week: Enos 1:1-8, 21-27

Enos 1:4-5 "And my soul
_ _ _ _ _ _ _ _ _; and I kneeled down
before my Maker and I prayed unto him in
mighty prayer ... all the day long did I cry unto
him; yea, and when night came I did raise my
_ _ _ _ _ high that it reached the
_ _ _ _ _ _ _ _. And there came a voice
unto me, saying: Enos, thy sins are forgiven
thee, and thou shalt be _ _ _ _ _ _ _."

BAPTISMAL COVENANTS:
I Will Follow Jesus and Serve Others

#10

SEARCH & PONDER CHALLENGE:
Read This Week: Mosiah 2:1-18

Mosiah 2:17-18 "And behold, I tell you these
things that ye may learn _ _ _ _ _ _ _; that
ye may learn that when ye are in the
_ _ _ _ _ _ _ _ of your fellow beings ye
are only in the service of your _ _ _.
Behold, ye have called me your king; and if I,
whom ye call your king, do _ _ _ _ _ _ to
serve you, then ought not ye to labor to
_ _ _ _ _ _ one another?"

MISSIONARY: #11

I Will Be Valiant and Tell Others About Jesus

SEARCH & PONDER CHALLENGE:
Read This Week: Mosiah 11:1-2, 20-21,
26-29; Mosiah 12:1-9; and Mosiah 17

Mosiah 16:14-15
"Therefore, if ye __ __ __ __ __ the law of
Moses [the 10 Commandments], also teach that
it is a __ __ __ __ __ __ of those things which
are to come--Teach them that redemption
cometh through __ __ __ __ __ __ the Lord,
who is the very Eternal Father Amen."

BAPTISM: #12

I Will Keep My Baptismal Covenants

SEARCH & PONDER CHALLENGE:
Read This Week: Mosiah 18:1-11 and
Mosiah 18:30-35

Mosiah 18:10 "If this be the desire of your
__ __ __ __ __ __ ... [to be] baptized in the
name of the __ __ __ __, as a witness before
him that ye have entered into a covenant with
him, that ye will __ __ __ __ __ him and keep
his commandments, that he may pour out his
__ __ __ __ __ __ more abundantly upon you."

ADVERSITY: #13

My Faith in Jesus Christ will Help Me

SEARCH & PONDER CHALLENGE:
Read This Week: Mosiah 21:6-16 and
Mosiah 24:10-15

Mosiah 24:15 "The burdens which were
__ __ __ __ upon Alma and his brethren were
made __ __ __ __ __; yea, the Lord did
__ __ __ __ __ __ __ __ __ __ them that they
could __ __ __ __ up their burdens with
__ __ __ __, and they did submit cheerfully and
with patience to all the will of the Lord."

REPENTANCE: #14

I Can Live in Heaven

SEARCH & PONDER CHALLENGE:
Read This Week: Mosiah 27:10-24

Mosiah 27:24

"For, said he, I have __ __ __ __ __ __ __ __ __
of my __ __ __ __, and have been
__ __ __ __ __ __ __ __ of the __ __ __ __;
behold I am __ __ __ __ of the Spirit."

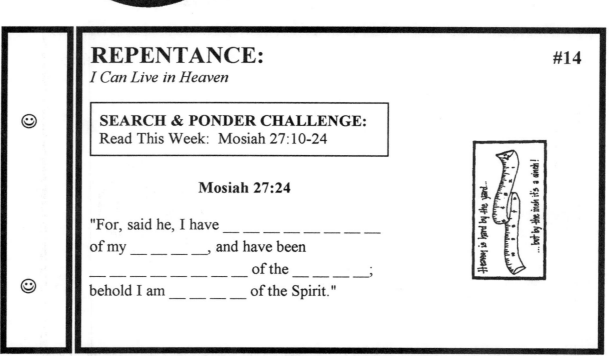

OBEDIENCE: #15
I Will Obey Like Alma & Amulek

SEARCH & PONDER CHALLENGE:
Read This Week: Alma 8:14-20

Alma 8:15 "Blessed art thou, Alma; therefore, lift up thy head and __ __ __ __ __ __ __ , for thou hast great cause to rejoice; for thou hast been __ __ __ __ __ __ __ __ in keeping the __ __ __ __ __ __ __ __ __ __ __ __ of God from the time which thou receivedst thy first message from him. Behold, I am he that delivered it to you." [message from an angel of the Lord].

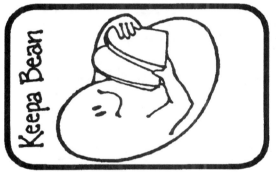

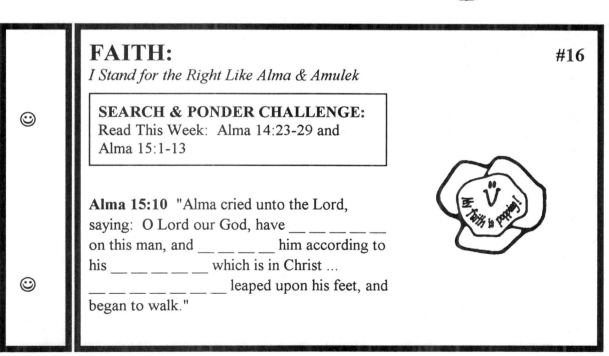

FAITH: #16
I Stand for the Right Like Alma & Amulek

SEARCH & PONDER CHALLENGE:
Read This Week: Alma 14:23-29 and
Alma 15:1-13

Alma 15:10 "Alma cried unto the Lord, saying: O Lord our God, have __ __ __ __ __ on this man, and __ __ __ __ him according to his __ __ __ __ __ which is in Christ ... __ __ __ __ __ __ __ leaped upon his feet, and began to walk."

MISSIONARY: #17
I Will Share My Testimony of Jesus Christ

SEARCH & PONDER CHALLENGE:
Read This Week: Alma 17:19-25, 18:8-40

Alma 18:34-35 "Ammon said ... I am a man; and a man in the beginning was created after the image of __ __ __, and I am called by his __ __ __ __ Spirit to __ __ __ __ __ these things unto this people, that they may be brought to a knowledge of that which is just and __ __ __ __; And ... that Spirit dwelleth in me, which giveth me knowledge, and also power according to my __ __ __ __ __ and desires which are in God."

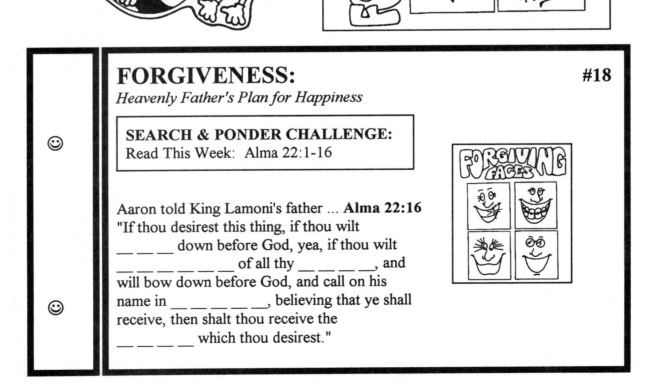

FORGIVENESS: #18
Heavenly Father's Plan for Happiness

SEARCH & PONDER CHALLENGE:
Read This Week: Alma 22:1-16

Aaron told King Lamoni's father ... **Alma 22:16** "If thou desirest this thing, if thou wilt __ __ __ down before God, yea, if thou wilt __ __ __ __ __ __ of all thy __ __ __ __, and will bow down before God, and call on his name in __ __ __ __ __, believing that ye shall receive, then shalt thou receive the __ __ __ __ which thou desirest."

COVENANTS: #19
I Can Keep Sacred Promises

SEARCH & PONDER CHALLENGE:
Read This Week: Alma 24:6-27

Alma 24:19 "When the Lamanites were
brought to __ __ __ __ __ __ and to know
the __ __ __ __ __, they were firm, and would
suffer even unto __ __ __ __ __ rather than
commit __ __ __; and thus we see that they
__ __ __ __ __ __ their __ __ __ __ __ __ __
of peace, or they buried the weapons of war, for
__ __ __ __ __."

TRUTH: #20
I Can Know the Truth and Follow Jesus

SEARCH & PONDER CHALLENGE:
Read This Week: Alma 30:12-18 and
Alma 30:37-56, 60

Alma 30:8 "For thus saith the scripture:
__ __ __ __ __ __ ye this day, whom ye will
serve."

Sunshine CTR Verse (shown right) Reads:
*"The more you choose the right the happier
you become. The happier you become, the
more your light shines."*

WORSHIP:

I Will Be Humble and Help

#21

SEARCH & PONDER CHALLENGE:
Read This Week: Alma 31:8-25 and Alma 34:17-29

Alma 34:17, 19, 26 "Therefore may God grant unto you, my brethren, that ye may begin to exercise your __ __ __ __ __ unto repentance, that ye begin to call upon his holy name, that he would have mercy upon you; Yea, __ __ __ __ __ __ yourselves, and continue in __ __ __ __ __ __ unto him ... ye must pour out your souls in your closets, and your secret places."

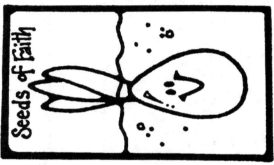

FAITH:

I Will Plant and Grow Seeds of Faith

#22

SEARCH & PONDER CHALLENGE:
Read This Week: Alma 32:21-22, 26-28, 40-43; and 33:14-23

Alma 32:21, 27-28 "Faith is not to have a __ __ __ __ __ __ __ __ knowledge of things; therefore if ye have faith ye __ __ __ __ for things which are not seen, which are true ... If ye will ... experiment upon my words, and exercise a particle of faith, yea, even if ye ... desire to believe, let that desire work in you, even until ye believe ... my words ... a seed may be planted in your __ __ __ __ __ ..."

SCRIPTURE CHALLENGE CARDS for lessons #19 and #20

SCRIPTURES: #23
Scriptures Guide Me to My Heavenly Home

SEARCH & PONDER CHALLENGE:
Read This Week: Alma 37:33-47 and Alma
38:1-12

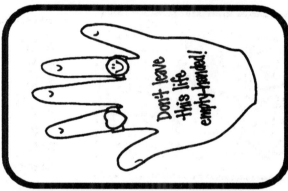

Alma 37:44 "For behold, it is as easy to give
__ __ __ __ __ to the __ __ __ __ __ of Christ, which
will __ __ __ __ __ __ to you a straight
__ __ __ __ __ __ __ to eternal bliss, as it was
for our fathers to give heed to this
__ __ __ __ __ __ __ __, which would point unto
them a straight course to the promised land."

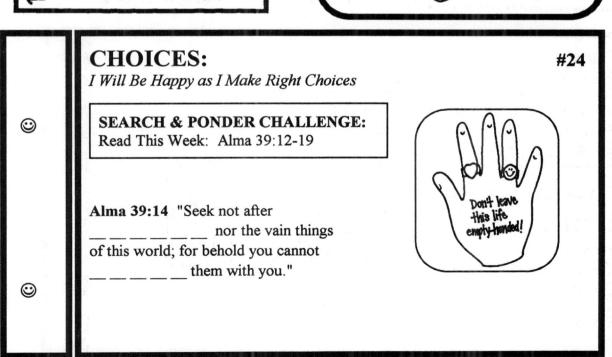

CHOICES: #24
I Will Be Happy as I Make Right Choices

SEARCH & PONDER CHALLENGE:
Read This Week: Alma 39:12-19

Alma 39:14 "Seek not after
__ __ __ __ __ __ nor the vain things
of this world; for behold you cannot
__ __ __ __ __ __ them with you."

ARMOR OF GOD

#25

Can Protect Me From Evil

SEARCH & PONDER CHALLENGE:
Read This Week: Alma 43:41-54 and
Alma 44:1-4

Alma 43:45 "The Nephites were inspired by a
better _ _ _ _ _ _, for they were not fighting for
monarchy nor power but they were fighting for their
_ _ _ _ _ _ and their liberties, their
_ _ _ _ _ _ and their _ _ _ _ _ _ _ _ _ _,
and their all, yea, for their rites of
_ _ _ _ _ _ _ _ and their _ _ _ _ _ _ _."

FREEDOM:

#26

I Stand for Right and Resist Evil

SEARCH & PONDER CHALLENGE:
Read This Week: Alma 48:11-13, 17-18

Alma 48:15 "If they were _ _ _ _ _ _ _ _ _ _
in keeping the commandments of God ... he would
_ _ _ _ _ _ _ _ them in the land."
Alma 48:17 "If all men had been, and were, and ever
would be, like unto _ _ _ _ _ _ _, behold, the
very powers of hell would have been shaken forever;
yea, the devil would never have _ _ _ _ _ _ over
the hearts of the children of men."

RIGHTEOUSNESS: #27
I Will Honor My Parents

SEARCH & PONDER CHALLENGE:
Read This Week: Alma 53:16-21
Alma 56:45-48   Alma 57:25-27

Alma 53:20-21   "And they were all young men, and they were exceedingly
_ _ _ _ _ _ _ _ _ for _ _ _ _ _ _ _ _ _,
and also for strength and activity; but behold, this was not all--they were men who were
_ _ _ _ at all times in whatsoever thing they were _ _ _ _ _ _ _ _ _ _."

CHOOSE THE RIGHT: #28
I Will Live the Teachings of Jesus

SEARCH & PONDER CHALLENGE:
Read This Week: Helaman 5:12

Helaman 5:12   "It is upon the _ _ _ _ _ of our Redeemer, who is _ _ _ _ _ _ _, the Son of God, that ye must _ _ _ _ _ _ your foundation ... whereon if men build they cannot _ _ _ _."

PROPHETS *Guide Me*

#29

SEARCH & PONDER CHALLENGE:
Read This Week: Helaman 8:25-28 and
Helaman 9

Helaman 8:19 "And now I would that ye
should know, that even since the days of
_ _ _ _ _ _ _ there have been many
prophets that have _ _ _ _ _ _ _ _ _
these things; yea, behold, the prophet
_ _ _ _ _ did testify boldly; for the which
he was slain."

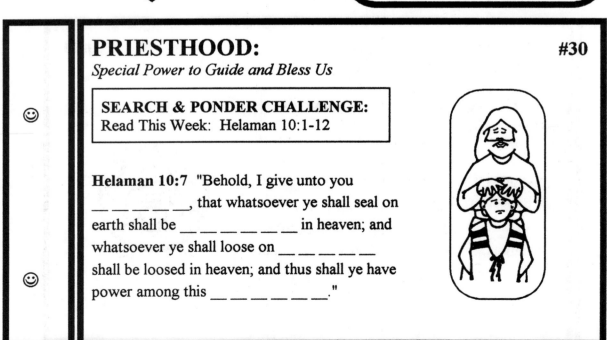

PRIESTHOOD:

#30

Special Power to Guide and Bless Us

SEARCH & PONDER CHALLENGE:
Read This Week: Helaman 10:1-12

Helaman 10:7 "Behold, I give unto you
_ _ _ _ _, that whatsoever ye shall seal on
earth shall be _ _ _ _ _ _ in heaven; and
whatsoever ye shall loose on _ _ _ _ _
shall be loosed in heaven; and thus shall ye have
power among this _ _ _ _ _ _."

SCRIPTURE CHALLENGE CARDS for lessons #19 and #20

PROPHETS   #31
Tell Me About the Life and Mission of Jesus

SEARCH & PONDER CHALLENGE:
Read This Week: Helaman 14:1-14
Helaman 14:20-31

Helaman 14:13   "And if ye
_ _ _ _ _ _ _ _ _on his name ye will
_ _ _ _ _ _ _ of all your
_ _ _ _ _, that thereby ye may have a
_ _ _ _ _ _ _ _ _ of them through
his merits."

SIGNS   #32
Can Strengthen My Testimony of Jesus

SEARCH & PONDER CHALLENGE:
Read This Week: 3 Nephi 1:4-15, 19-22

3 Nephi 1:20-21   "And it had come to pass,
yea, all things, every whit, according to the
_ _ _ _ _ of the prophets. And it came to
pass also that a new _ _ _ _ did
_ _ _ _ _ _, according to the word."

TESTIMONY: #33
I Have a Testimony of Jesus Christ

SEARCH & PONDER CHALLENGE:
Read This Week: 3 Nephi 11

3 Nephi 11:33 "And whoso
_ _ _ _ _ _ _ _ _ _ in me, and is
_ _ _ _ _ _ _ _ _, the same shall be
_ _ _ _ _ _; and they are they who shall
inherit the kingdom of _ _ _."

BEATITUDES: #34
Jesus Taught the Nephites How to Be Happy

SEARCH & PONDER CHALLENGE:
Read This Week: 3 Nephi 12:3-24, 39-48

3 Nephi 12:15-16 "Behold, do men light a
_ _ _ _ _ _ _ and put it under a bushel?
Nay, but on a candlestick, and it giveth
_ _ _ _ _ _ to all that are in the
_ _ _ _ _ _; Therefore, let your light so
_ _ _ _ _ _ before this people, that they
may see your good _ _ _ _ _ and glorify
your Father who is in _ _ _ _ _ _ _."

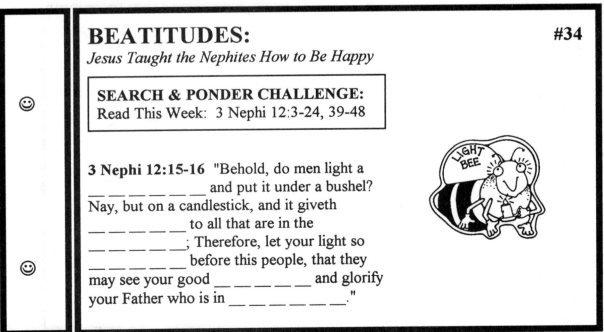

LOVE:
#35

Jesus and Heavenly Father Love Me

SEARCH & PONDER CHALLENGE:
Read This Week: 3 Nephi 17

3 Nephi 17:19-21 "Jesus spake unto them: ...
Blessed are ye because of your __ __ __ __ __.
And now behold, my joy is full. And when he
had said these words, he wept, and the
multitude bare record of it, and he took their
little __ __ __ __ __ __ __ __, one by one, and
__ __ __ __ __ __ __ them, and
__ __ __ __ __ __ __ unto the Father for them."

SACRAMENT:
#36

I Will Remember Jesus

SEARCH & PONDER CHALLENGE:
Read This Week: 3 Nephi 18:1-14

3 Nephi 18:14, 16 "Therefore
__ __ __ __ __ __ __ are ye if ye shall
keep my commandments, which the Father hath
commanded me that I should give unto you ...
Behold I am the __ __ __ __ __;
I have set an __ __ __ __ __ __ __ for you."

PRAYER

#37

Will Protect Me From Temptation

> **SEARCH & PONDER CHALLENGE:**
> Read This Week: 3 Nephi 18:18-25 and
> Alma 13:28-29

Alma 13:28 "Humble yourselves before the Lord, and call on his holy name, and __ __ __ __ __ and pray continually, that ye may not be __ __ __ __ __ __ __ __ above that which ye can bear, and thus be __ __ __ by the Holy Spirit, becoming __ __ __ __ __ __ , meek, submissive, patient, full of love, and all long-suffering ... having faith on the Lord."

I'll pray morning and night to keep heaven in sight!

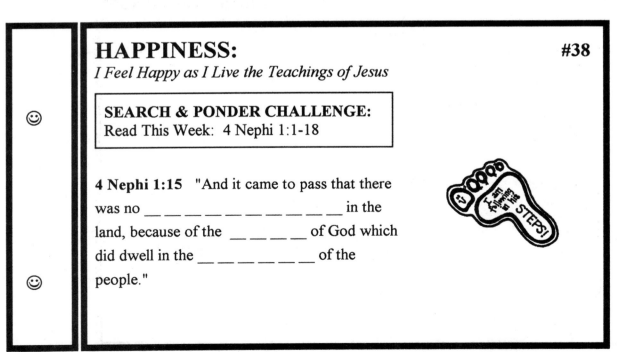

HAPPINESS:

#38

I Feel Happy as I Live the Teachings of Jesus

> **SEARCH & PONDER CHALLENGE:**
> Read This Week: 4 Nephi 1:1-18

4 Nephi 1:15   "And it came to pass that there was no __ __ __ __ __ __ __ __ __ __ __ in the land, because of the __ __ __ __ of God which did dwell in the __ __ __ __ __ __ of the people."

HONOR: *I Will Be True to the Teachings of Jesus* #39

SEARCH & PONDER CHALLENGE:
Read This Week: Mormon 1:1-7, 13-19

Mormon 3:2-3 "The Lord did say unto me: Cry unto this people--__ __ __ __ __ __ ye, and come unto me, and be ye baptized, and build up again my church, and ye shall be spared. And I did cry unto this people, but it was in vain; and they did not realize that it was the Lord that had __ __ __ __ __ __ them, and granted unto them a chance for repentance ... behold they did __ __ __ __ __ __ their hearts against the Lord their God."

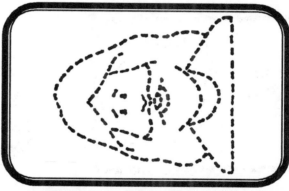

HOLY GHOST: #40
I Can Be Worthy of His Spirit

SEARCH & PONDER CHALLENGE:
Read This Week: Ether 3:6-16

Ether 4:11 "He that believeth these things which I have spoken, him will I __ __ __ __ __ with the manifestations of my __ __ __ __ __ __ __, and __ __ shall know and bear record. For because of my __ __ __ __ __ __ __ he shall know that these things are __ __ __ __; for it persuadeth men to do __ __ __ __."

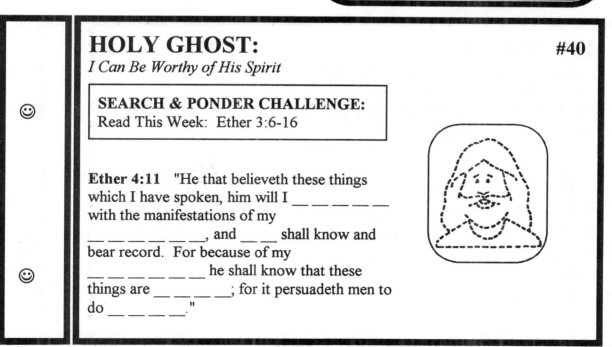

PROPHETS:

#41

I Will Listen to the Prophet to
Stay in the Light

> **SEARCH & PONDER CHALLENGE:**
> Read This Week: Ether 13:13-22; 15:33-34

Ether 13:13 "Great and marvelous were the prophecies of __ __ __ __ __; but they esteemed him as naught, and __ __ __ __ him out; and he __ __ __ himself in the cavity of a rock by day, and by night he went forth viewing the things which should __ __ __ __ upon the people."

CHARITY:

#42

I Choose the Pure Love of Christ

> **SEARCH & PONDER CHALLENGE:**
> Read: Moroni 1; 7:5-19, 43-48; 8:14

Moroni 7:45 "And charity __ __ __ __ __ __ __ __ __ __ long, and is __ __ __ __ __, and envieth not, and is not __ __ __ __ __ __ __ up, seeketh not her own, is not easily provoked, thinketh no evil, and rejoiceth not in __ __ __ __ __ __ __ __ but rejoiceth in the __ __ __ __ __, beareth all things, believeth all things, __ __ __ __ __ __ all things, endureth all things."

FAITH: #43
I Will Be Strong in Faith

> **SEARCH & PONDER CHALLENGE:**
> Read This Week: Ether 12:6-22, 41

Ether 12:12-13 "If there be no _ _ _ _ _ _
among the children of men God can do _ _
miracle among them; wherefore he showed not
himself until _ _ _ _ _ their faith. Behold,
it was the faith of _ _ _ _ and
_ _ _ _ _ _ that caused the prison to
tumble to the earth."

TESTIMONY: #44
The Book of Mormon Promise

> **SEARCH & PONDER CHALLENGE:**
> Read This Week: Moroni 10:1-5

Moroni 10:4-5 "And when ye shall receive these
things, I would exort you that ye would _ _ _
God, the Eternal Father, in the name of Christ, if
these things are not true; and if ye shall ask with a
sincere _ _ _ _ _, with real intent, having
_ _ _ _ _ in Christ, he will manifest the truth
of it unto you, by the power of the Holy Ghost. And
by the power of the Holy Ghost ye may know the
_ _ _ _ _ of all things."

EASTER: #45
Book of Mormon Testifies of Resurrection

SEARCH & PONDER CHALLENGE:
Read This Week: 3 Nephi 11:8-17

2 Nephi 9:18-22 "The righteous, the saints of
the __ __ __ __ One of Israel, they who have
believed ... who have endured the crosses of the
world ... shall __ __ __ __ __ __ __ the
kingdom of __ __ __ ... and their joy shall be
forever. The Holy One of Israel (Jesus Christ)
... delivered his saints from that awful monster
the devil ... he suffereth the pains of all men ...
that the resurrection ... pass upon all men."

CHRISTMAS   #46
Book of Mormon a Second Witness of Jesus

SEARCH & PONDER CHALLENGE:
Read This Week: 1 Nephi 11:12-24 and
2 Nephi 29:8

1 Nephi 11:14-15, 18, 20 "And it came to pass
that I saw the __ __ __ __ __ __ __ open; and
an __ __ __ __ __ came down and stood before
me; and he said unto me: Nephi, what
beholdest thou? And I said unto him:
A virgin ... whom thou seest is the mother of
the Son of __ __ __, after the manner of the
flesh ... bearing a child in her __ __ __ __."

My
SCRIPTURE
Activity Notebook
I'm Trying to Be Like Jesus

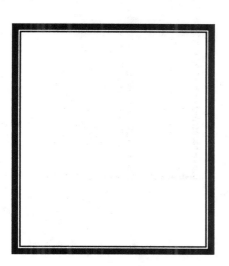

Picture of Me at Age _____

I will SEARCH, PONDER, AND PRAY,
and try to be more like Jesus each day.
I Will Read the Scriptures Daily.

My Name:

My Teacher's Name:

My Gospel-in-Action Goals:

ARTICLES OF FAITH Memorization Checklist:
1 ☐ *2* ☐ *3* ☐ *4* ☐ *5* ☐ *6* ☐ *7* ☐ *8* ☐ *9* ☐ *10* ☐ *11* ☐ *12* ☐ *13* ☐

Preview of *File Folder FAMILY HOME EVENINGS*
You'll find 12 Themes to Use for Primary Lessons,
Primary Sharing Time, and Family Home Evening
by Ross and Guymon-King

THEMES:
HEAVENLY TREASURES: Follow the
Straight and Narrow Path
SEEDS OF FAITH: My Testimony is Growing
ANGEL TELLS OF TWO BIRTHS: John and Jesus
LET'S CELEBRATE the Birth of Jesus
CREATING ME: I'm Trying to Be Like Jesus
FISHERS OF MEN: Jesus Choose 12 Apostles
BLESSED BEATITUDES: Jesus Gave the Sermon on the Mount
THE GIFTS HE GAVE: Tell Me the Stories of Jesus
SERVICE WITH A SMILE: Jesus Performed Miracles
CHOOSE THE RIGHT: Jesus Is Our Light
CAPTAIN OF OUR SHIP: Jesus Is Our Life Savior
IN HIS STEPS: Spotlighting the Life of Jesus

Here's a Sample of One File
Folder Family Home Evening

BLESSED BEATITUDES:
Jesus Gave the
Sermon on the Mount
Show-and-Tell (shown right)

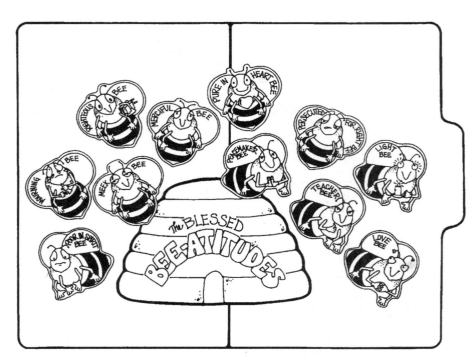

ACTIVITY:
<u>Bee-atitude Blockbuster</u> quiz game (shown above)

THOUGHT TREAT: <u>Honey Buzz Taffy</u> and
<u>Bee-atitude Bagels</u>
(shown right)

Mary H. Ross, Author and
Jennette Guymon-King, Illustrator
are the creators of

PRIMARY PARTNERS BOOKS & CD-ROMS
Lesson Match Activities and More:
Nursery and Age 3 (Sunbeams) Vol. 1 + CD-ROM
Nursery and Age 3 (Sunbeams) Vol. 2 + CD-ROM
CTR A and CTR B Ages 4-7 + CD-ROM
Book of Mormon Ages 8-11 + CD-ROM
Old Testament Ages 8-11
New Testament Ages 8-11 + CD-ROM
Doctrine and Covenants Ages 8-11
Achievement Days, Girls Ages 8-11
Sharing Time: Faith in Jesus Christ + CD-ROM
Sharing Time: Baptismal Covenants + CD-ROM
Primary Partners: Clip-Art on CD-ROM (500 images)
Primary Partners Singing Fun! + CD-ROM

FAMILY HOME EVENING BOOKS & CD-ROMS:
File Folder Family Home Evenings + CD-ROM
Home-spun Fun Family Home Evenings 1 + CD-ROM
Home-spun Fun Family Home Evenings 2 + CD-ROM

YOUNG WOMEN BOOKS & CD-ROMS:
Young Women Fun-tastic! Activities Manual 3
Young Women Fun-tastic! Activities Manual 1 + CD-ROM
My Fun-tastic! Personal Progress Planner and Journal (Beehive 1 and 2)

MARY H. ROSS, Author
Mary Ross (shown left) is an energetic mother, and has been a Primary teacher and Achievement Days leader. She loves to help children and young women have a good time while they learn. She has studied acting, modeling, and voice. Her varied interests include writing, creating activities and children's parties, and cooking. Mary and her husband, Paul, live with their daughter, Jennifer, in Sandy, Utah.

JENNETTE GUYMON-KING, Illustrator
Jennette Guymon-King (shown right) has studied graphic arts and illustration at Utah Valley State College and the University of Utah. She served a mission to Japan. Jennette enjoys sports, reading, cooking, art, gardening, and freelance illustrating. Jennette and her husband, Clayton, live in Riverton, Utah. They are the proud parents of their daughter Kayla Mae.

Here's another fun-filled, information-packed book focusing on each of the Achievement Days goals. Leaders, you will never be at a loss when it comes to choosing activities or projects to make goal achievement memorable.

You can make these activities simple or elaborate. Whatever your choice, you'll all be in for a great time! Start each activity with an invitation to create interest, for a year's worth of "go"al get 'em activities!

YOU'LL FIND:

MOTIVATIONAL PARTIES
Pop Into the Future!
Soar to Success!
Dad and Me Western Jamboree
Mom and Miss Pig-nic
Burstin' with Pride!

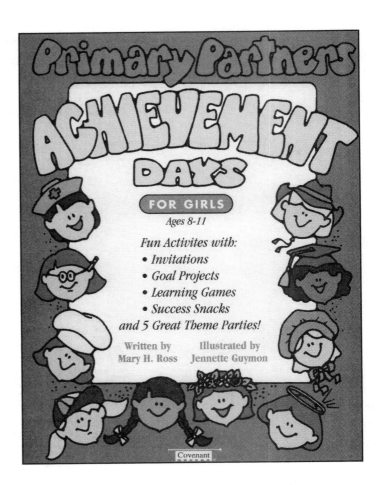

Primary Partners
ACHIEVEMENT DAYS

FOR GIRLS
Ages 8-11

Fun Activites with:
- *Invitations*
- *Goal Projects*
- *Learning Games*
- *Success Snacks*
and 5 Great Theme Parties!

Written by   Illustrated by
Mary H. Ross   Jennette Guymon

Covenant

GOAL ACTIVITIES

ARTS & CRAFTS
Let's Make Pop-ups!
You're On Stage!

EDUCATION & SCHOLARSHIP
Wishin' in the Wishin' Well
Be a Jelly Bean Reader

FAMILY HISTORY
My Family Tree and Me
Journal Jazz!

FAMILY SKILLS
I Can Cook!
Super Sitter Basics

HEALTH & PERSONAL GROOMING
An Apple-a-Day the Healthy Way
Closet Class!

SPIRITUALITY
B.E.A.R.S.
(Be Enthusiastic About Reading Scriptures)
Home Sweet Home

OUTDOOR FUN & SKILLS
Ladybug Gardening Fun!
Nature Photo-rama!

PERSONAL PREPAREDNESS
I Can Eat an Elephant!
My Cents-able Savings Plan

SAFETY & EMERGENCY PREPAREDNESS
I Can Be Safe
First Aid Station

SERVICE & CITIZENSHIP
Hop to it! Service
That Grand Old Flag!

HOSPITALITY
Friends Forever!
Let's Be Pen Pals!

SPORTS & PHYSICAL FITNESS
Three Cheers for Good Sport!
Freta Frog's Fitness Fun